Gus Salbodou
5-88

P 44   Ordained ministry

P 106   Christian Faith
         "Koinonia"
  108   ARCIC - church unity
  109   Kingdom of God

The Episcopal Church In Crisis

"John Booty has offered the Episcopal Church an opportunity to reflect on its most recent history. Such a reflection can only facilitate the process of identity seeking and thus move us forward in mission."

—Richard F. Grein
Bishop of Kansas

"Must reading for those wanting to place in perspective the dynamic and interrelated developments in the life of the Episcopal Church in the recent past. His book enables the reader to place together the pieces of a jigsaw puzzle of the recent past into a picture of the Episcopal Church today."

—Pamela P. Chinnis
Vice President, House of Deputies

"Bringing together such widely disparate topics as the Ecumenical Movement, the Church and the Vietnam War, the Charismatic Movement, and others, and exploring their relations to one another is a major feat of scholarship and creative thinking, and results in a book which the whole Church needs to read, mark, learn and inwardly digest."

—David B. Reed
Bishop of Kentucky

"Read these pages, be ye Episcopalian or not, ... Booty gives us the portrait of a church in crisis ... the story of a pulsing, problematic, all-too-human church and somehow-divine Church in action."

—Martin E. Marty
University of Chicago

Other Cowley Titles by John Booty

The Christ We Know
Meditating On Four Quartets
Three Anglican Divines On Prayer

THE
EPISCOPAL CHURCH
IN
CRISIS

John Booty

1 9 8 8

Cowley Publications
Cambridge, Massachusetts

Published by Cowley Publications.
International Standard Book No.: 0-936384-57-3

Library of Congress Cataloging-in-Publication Data

Booty, John E.
    The Episcopal Church in crisis.
    "Originally presented as the Brennan lectures for
1986"—Pref.
    Bibliography: p.
    Includes index.
    1. Episcopal Church—History—20th century.
2. Anglican Communion—United States—History—20th
century. 3. United States—Church history—20th
century. I. Title.
BX5882.b66 1988   283'.73   88-370
ISBN 0-936384-57-3

Cowley Publications
980 Memorial Drive
Cambridge, MA 02138

Acknowledgments

The chapters in this book were originally presented as the Brennan Lectures for 1986. Made possible by a bequest from Dr. Robert Emory Brennan (1879–1969), the Brennan Lectures are provided for the continuing education of the clergy of the Diocese of Kentucky and are open to clergy and laity of all denominations. I am grateful to the Commission on Ministry for the invitation to present these lectures and to the Reverend E. Benjamin Sanders, chairman of the commission, for his arrangements and for providing gracious introductions. My wife and I thank the Bishop of Kentucky and his wife, for their hospitality. I am especially grateful for Bishop Reed's comments and suggestions, as well as for all of the other comments and suggestions that came out of discussions following each lecture. Finally, I wish to thank the Reverend Professor Donald S. Armentrout for his assistance and support.

John Booty

Contents

The Ecumenical Movement and the Nature of the Church
The Episcopal Church and Planet Earth

Foreword

by Martin Marty

We study history in order to intervene in history. That formula by two late great church historians motivates John Booty to tell this story. We study history in order to act. That notion runs against the image many have of history. They react against badly-taught high school history courses or texts which somehow achieve the unimaginably difficult: they make history dull. They drone or ramble about dates and obscure events until their students or readers forget that these events involved passionate, perverse, heroic, stumbling, saintly mortals. Booty's characters in this book have something to tell us, whether in their stumblings or saintlinesses. As we learn about their course, we may learn how to intervene.

History is about the past, and the past is gone, isn't it? As I read these pages, paragraphs about times in which, like the author, I have personal memories, it occurred to me how irretrievable the past seems to be. When he told of his days in the fifties as a curate, times when his parish shepherded seven hundred children in church school, I thought of my own experience with the same number in a suburban congregation. After I left, as the baby boom crested, my successor pastor was confirming as many as one hundred children per year. His successor, a no less capable pastor than his two predecessors, tending to people no less faithful than ours, probably confirms ten children in a good year.

What went wrong? Did the Gospel dry up? Did a bomb hit the suburb? Does no one care about the transmission of faith and knowledge? No, not exactly. The people who replaced our

generation are not marrying or else marrying late, or having few
children or retiring early or moving often or spending weekends
at their lakeside place and in general not providing a cohort for
faithful people to train in Christian ways at church school. The
past that was the 1950s is gone. Booty helps recover it, for those
who lived through it; he describes a world that must seem fantastic or remote to those who did not. The 1950s are longer ago,
so far as church styles are concerned, than the 1850s. The fifties
was the only decade when "everything worked" in church life.
To use it as a measure for later decades is defeating. We study
history to be liberated from history. Booty is a liberator. He shows
us that the past is a foreign country where they do things differently. We can visit it on these pages, but we cannot live there
again even if we wish to.

The past is past. No, it isn't. The other strong impression that
came to me as I read this book in manuscript form is to notice
that it lives, how it lives. By this I mean, as some sages who have
thought about history remind us, that the past is here to shape
us, haunt us, give us clues for guidance. John Booty spends some
time talking about how the study of history provides an identity.
Episcopalians do not "make up" the story that constitutes their
church and their community life (though at times in this story it
looks as if some of them are!) No, they are a community of
memory and hope. Their memories are not all about the creed-
making early Christian centuries or the sixteenth century in
England. Recent memories also provide group identity which,
he reminds us, one needs if there is to be action today.

A study of the past guides us? I let that slip in, and now wish
to qualify it. The story an historian invents about traces left from
past events is a creation; someone who has left the Episcopal
Church in reaction against Prayer Book change or the ordination
of women would tell the story differently. Such a person would
probably draw different lessons and offer different implicit
guidance than does John Booty. Neither can predict the future;
neither could be sure about how to apply lessons. Still, by feed-

ing group identity and motivating group action, the historian can describe roads taken and not taken, good past choices and bad ones. And one can get some sense of bearing and direction from such a narrative.

Contemporary history, the story of the recent past, offers challenges which the author of this book first takes cognizance of and then accepts as a challenge. It is one thing to tell the story of the remote past, after most documents have been lost, after almost all have been picked over. It is another matter to sort out details from a documentary blizzard—there have not yet been enough burned libraries, destroyed attics—and find the significance in stories about people still alive or about people we remember.

Even the emotional investment is different. A good historian can get me to weep about what Tennyson's *Ulysses* showed were "old, unhappy, far-off things, and battles long ago." Yet I relate differently to foreign folk from millennia ago than I do to my own parents and my own younger self, and so do readers of books like this. One emotion that Booty may not have set out to evoke, but which overcame me, was sadness—though I am not Episcopalian. Was it in his manner? No, it is in the stuff of history. At our house we say, "There are no happy memories; there are only some memories of some happy events." Look through your family photograph album from the 1950s. There you or your parents are pictured observing marriages and baptisms, vacations and celebrations. They, or you, are lifting glasses in toasts, giggling before the fire, stiffly posing on the front porch, back when there were porches.

Then you look again. Dad left her. Mom died of cancer. Uncle Raymond? Oh, oh, oh—he was the party man, but they told us of his suicide after he failed in business. Alcohol took that one. She never lived up to her promise. He had a happy, eventful, fulfilling life: too bad I cannot reach him any longer to tell him what he meant to me. There are so many unfinished steps toward happiness, so many inevitable steps toward tragedy. The events were happy, but they induce sad memories.

6

pages, be ye Episcopalian or not, and find out how
o̶i̶ sense of memory speaking sadly will come. Yet
Booty is ꓫ a mopey type, nor does he dwell on sadnesses. He
also knows the purgative power of history. It can help disabuse
us of notions that the past represents "the good old days." He
shows how God's faithful people endure, adapt, persevere, use
Plan B, and all that compensatorily cheers us. I even found it con-
soling to see his title about "crisis" in the singular. I see so many
crises that I find it hard to grasp handles for dealing with them.
It is therapeutic and motivating to have his help give shape, find
a *Gestalt*, a whole, by which one can address the times as crisis.

In these days of Lutheran-Episcopal ententes, of "interim
shared eucharist," may I import a line of Martin Luther that ap-
plies well to the broken church in crisis, the one that still somehow can judge and save people? Luther said that God rides the
lame horse, God carves the rotten wood. Never did God wait for
the perfect carrier, the unblemished raw material, in order to act
in history. Booty gives us the portrait of a church in crisis which
has passed on crises and resources.

It has not been easy to write several pages about the effects of
his book, the problems the author faced, without getting into the
plot. But I resisted the temptation. It would take a book of his
length to provide informed and helpful comment on an event-
by-event basis. It would take a more informed reader than I to
be able to pick away at his details. And it would take a ruder person than I to butt in on his plot, to reveal his details. For now, let
me be content to remind myself that anyone who has been a pastor in the presence of seven hundred church school children in
the long ago has earned the right to enough serenity that he can
pursue the work of the church historian. He needed that serenity
and perspective in order to give us this story of a pulsing,
problematic, all-too-human church and somehow-divine
Church in action. Turn the page, please.

Martin E. Marty
The University of Chicago

Introduction

Prolegomena

There is a sense in which the recent past is too close to be objectively assessed. Our memories are full of images, images that stir our emotions because they represent something of ourselves, some things not yet laid to rest in our own experience. We can speak of the "Cold War" dispassionately, but I am troubled as I remember the anxious search for a fall-out shelter in the midst of the Cuba Missile Crisis. We can speak learnedly of the technological revolution, but we know how we have been affected by it personally as we "boot-up" our computers and benefit from the existence of the "cat-scan." Our passions are aroused when we think of people humiliated and unemployed as a result of factory automation. As an historian I can analyze that dramatic moment in the civil rights movement when Rosa Parks refused to give up her seat to a white person on a bus in Montgomery, but I was there when the race riots broke out on a bridge in Detroit in 1943. I was there at the Lincoln Memorial when Martin Luther King, Jr. eloquently declared, "I have a dream." Having experienced the effects of injustice and violence, that dream was my dream too. The Vietnam War is now a subject for study in learned monographs, but I know a man haunted by memories of fear and death in "the big muddy." The recent past is still present to me and to countless numbers of persons still alive who shared that past.

I remember the boom-time of the Episcopal Church in the 1950s when as a young curate I strove to manage a Sunday school of 700 children and 70 teachers and substitutes. Terms such as "group dynamics," "parish life conferences," and "the Seabury

Plan," point to facets of my experience as a priest of the Episcopal Church engaged in parish ministry. Amidst the landmarks along the way I remember Jonathan Daniels dying in Alabama, John Fitzgerald Kennedy being assassinated in Dallas, and the Black Manifesto rocketing out of Detroit. There was the initial shock of radical theologians proclaiming "God is dead." There were conferences on liturgy sponsored by Associated Parishes and there was the exciting task of devising a liturgy as an adult class project, long before the appearance of books commonly known as Green, Zebra, and Proposed, long before the 1979 Book of Common Prayer. There are memories of John Hines and the Special Program, of Jack Allin and Venture in Mission, of Toronto 1963 and Mutual Responsibility and Interdependence in the Body of Christ, of COCU and Vatican II, conflict and confusion, confrontation and defection—memories all so vivid and personal as well as reflecting fragments and themes in the history of a people, a church and a nation. There is a sense in which the events of the 1950s, 60s, 70s, and 80s are too close to be objectively assessed.

It is, nevertheless, important to us both personally and socially, for the sake of our souls' health and the welfare of the church and the nation, that we review the events of the recent past both appreciatively and critically. And we can do it, for as close as those years are to us, they are past, a part of history. Ask any teenager about President Kennedy, Vietnam, or the moon-landing and you will know how long ago Kennedy was assassinated, the Vietnam War came to its inglorious end, and the first astronaut set foot on the uninviting surface of our lunar companion in space. Then too there is the fact that we live in a time of accelerating change. Arthur M. Schlesinger, Jr. has pointed out that humans have lived on earth for 800 lifetimes, most spent in caves. The last two lifetimes have seen more achieved scientifically and technologically than the previous 798. Says Schlesinger:

> The pace of change grows ever faster. A boy who saw the
> Wright brothers fly for a few seconds at Kitty Hawk in 1903

could have watched Apollo 11 land on the moon in 1969. The first rockets were launched in the 1920s; today astronauts roam outer space. The first electronic computer was built in 1946; today the world rushes from the mechanical into the electronic age. The double helix was first unveiled in 1953; today, biotechnology threatens to remake mankind. The first atomic bomb fell in 1945; today the world shudders under the threat of nuclear obliteration.[1]

This means that present events become past events more quickly while at the same time continuing, if only in memory, alive in our personal present. Furthermore, as the pace of change accelerates, the human agenda changes more rapidly and we are prone to forget more quickly that which occurred only yesterday. I remember how in one academic year at the Episcopal Theological School we were so involved in struggling with the meaning for us of the Black Manifesto that significant sums of money were pledged for use in the Black Economic Development Corporation. However, in the next academic year it was as if we had entirely forgotten what we had done; our agenda now concerned women's liberation and the Blacks at ETS were hurt and angry. Time and events were moving with accelerating speed.

More importantly, there is the way in which the past determines the present and the future. To move from one agenda to another without reflection on what has happened is to allow ourselves to be tyrannized by past events. If we are to deal meaningfully with current issues we must consider our past, both as individuals and as groups—churches and nations. The study of the past can liberate us for the future if it is done honestly and is not an exercise in mere antiquarianism. We study the past to establish contact with the life-line of our nation and the heritage of our church, and thereby to be enlightened. We study the past to locate the errors and the miscalculations that have resulted in further errors and miscalculations. Having located them we have a greater ability to control them and, where possible, to lay them to rest.

Thus to study the past is to engage in reform. Reform has two aspects, the one involving renewal of that which is essential to our being as God created us to be, the other necessitating disavowal and possibly eradication of that which is either non-essential and harmful, or else explicitly evil in relation to our vocation in the present and for the sake of future generations. If we were truly wise we would have a department of the national church dedicated to historical study, conservative in the best sense, liberating in relation to the essential conservation of our sacred heritage.

I say this by way of prolegomenon, admitting that what we shall be doing is difficult, even painful, while arguing that it is a vital necessity.

Organizing History

History is the study of the human past, a social science requiring organization. A chronology informs us what has happened year by year. Usually it is compiled on the basis of the importance of events as judged by the historian in relation to peers, but without any special pleading or limiting themes. History is different from chronology. It concerns the human story told in narrative form, organized in particular ways with an overt purpose. There are, thus, histories of particular aspects of human experience written from particular points of view: constitutional, economic, political, biographical, military, and ecclesiastical histories. Ecclesiastical history is the story of the church, as the name implies, and varies from history to history according to each particular church historian's interests and the way in which the historian perceives the church's concerns. Some ecclesiastical histories recount events with sparse, often veiled interpretations, some begin by stating the historian's particular aims and biases, and some are histories of doctrine, of theological controversies, of church parties and of particular persons and groups.

This venture in ecclesiastical history is governed by my concern for ecclesiology, for the church's self-understanding as a corporate entity expressed in concrete events and in reflection on those events. I have no qualms in beginning thus, for in my research and reflection I have determined that the self-understanding of the church provides a reasonable, cogent basis for consideration of virtually all of the important events in the life of the Episcopal Church from 1950 on—as I determine what is and what is not important according to my own interpretation and in relation to the judgments of others whom I respect. I admit to being anxiously concerned that leaders of the Episcopal Church too often base their understanding of the church on the opinions of others and of contemporary society as a whole, rather than on that which brought it to be and has sustained it through the years—the Holy Spirit of the one God made known through Jesus Christ.

Some might have preferred that the story be told from the perspective of some portion of the whole—civil rights or women's rights, church renewal or ecumenics, liturgics or mission. The need as I see it is for history that is inclusive, taking seriously the major movements of the time, observing their interaction, watching for signs and signals that not only help us to understand the past but enable us to go with courage into the future. Admittedly, I regard the study of ecclesiastical history as an important facet of the church's theological task. Thus regarding it, I see as one of its responsibilities that of showing the interrelationship of persons and things, institutions and movements, the dynamic interaction and mutual penetration of all the vital elements in the life of the people identified as the People of God.

The Pursuit of Identity

This study has been influenced by a concern to establish, as well as may be, the *identity* of the Episcopal Church. Stephen

Sykes has striven to locate the "identity" of Christianity, acknowledging his debt to the nineteenth century discussion of "the essence of Christianity." He writes that in speaking of the "identity
of Christianity" he has "meant, in all innocence, the enquiry into
what makes Christianity Christianity."[2] The quest for identity is
made both pressing and difficult by "the sheer diversity of forms
of Christianity." Furthermore, Sykes has discovered that Christianity is multifaceted. He writes:

> A simple way of appreciating this important fact is to recall
> the threefold medieval confession of sin in 'thought, word
> and deed'. Thinking, speaking and doing are, so to speak,
> theatres of the Christian warfare in which personal defeat
> may be suffered.

The Christian life thus involves "true thought, true speech, and
true action."

> The threefold nature of Christianity, roughly correspond-
> ing to the threefold theatre expounded above, but more
> particularly to the threefold office of Christ as prophet,
> priest, and king, is a thought upon which John Henry New-
> man briefly touches. 'Christianity is dogmatical, devotion-
> al, practical all at once'.[3]

It is not my intent to pursue Sykes' argument further other
than simply to note that the quest for identity is complex, and
that we cannot expect the identity we discern to be other than
diverse and multifaceted. I now refer, of course, to the quest for
the identity of the Episcopal Church from 1950 into the present,
which is one way of stating the aim of this book. That quest will
be pursued through the observation of the Episcopal Church in
relation to some events arising out of internal developments, out
of the church's response to developments in American society,
and out of the church's involvement in global issues and move-

ments. We shall also, in this quest, pay attention to the multi-faceted nature of Christianity, to thinking, speaking, and doing, which is to say to theology, worship and social action. And we shall not be surprised to find diversity. Indeed, a theme emerging from this study is that of "diversity in unity," for an important aspect of the life of the Episcopal Church is just that; thus the Episcopal Church itself is ecumenical, in a sense, and experiences the pain and joy involved in people of considerable diversity co- existing in a family, an intimate fellowship dedicated to reconciliation.

In this quest for the identity of the Episcopal Church we begin with a definition by John Knox of the universal church, a definition arising out of one of the focal events of the time, a definition which becomes for this study a hypothesis, a touchstone and guide, and an expression of essence or identity in ideal terms. We turn now to the setting in which that definition was set forth.

Chapter 1

The Episcopal Church as a Fellowship in the Love of God

The Pike Affair

The opening years of the 1960s were years of theological ferment and controversy. An article in *The New Yorker* described the emergence of radical theologians proclaiming the death of God. A series of books was published ranging from the scholarly to the popular, all drawing considerable attention to their authors. Among the scholarly books were J.A.T. Robinson's *Honest to God*, Paul Van Buren's *The Secular Meaning of the Gospel*, and Joseph Fletcher's *Situation Ethics*, to name but three, all by Anglicans, all quite different. Such works were attempts at relating received credal statements to ways of thinking in modern, technological society. Based on secular or naturalistic assumptions, the radical theologies of the 1960s challenged the viability of the dominant neo-orthodoxy of the church's leaders and were skeptical of meaningful discourse concerning ultimate values. Rigorously applying empirical tests prevalent in modern philosophy and science, the radicals tended to find God-talk by and large senseless and thus proclaimed, sometimes stridently, that God had died. What they meant was hotly debated, some arguing that like Paul Tillich in *Courage to Be*, by the death of God the radical theologians meant the death of the god of contemporary culture and so pointed toward the God beyond god. Others concluded that they meant simply that God was dead (without qualification). For most the death of God did not mean that Christianity was dead; it most obviously was not. Christians still had the historical Jesus and what Van Buren called "the contagion of Jesus," a force that grasps and transforms, and is thus in a limited sense supernatural. Such allowances did little to assuage the concern and anger of the tradition-minded conservatives in the church. They rightly sensed that the radical theologians were presenting a challenge, requiring some response. It was also apparent that the intensity of the challenge was due in large part to mass-media publicity, a phenomenon of the age.

James Pike's *A Time for Christian Candor* (1964) was a relatively late entry in the fray, but it provided a major focus of concern for many members of the Episcopal Church. It had been preceded by a sermon on the Trinity preached by the learned and provocative Bishop of California at Trinity Church, Wall Street, New York. That sermon fed fuel to the fire that was already flaring around the bishop's feet. In July 1965, a group of clergy from the diocese of Arizona charged that Pike had repudiated the doctrines of the Virgin Birth, the Incarnation, and the Trinity, and was therefore heretical. The charges were presented to the House of Bishops meeting at East Glacier, Montana, September 7–9, 1965. The Theological Committee of the House reported that Pike was not on trial and defended his right to engage in theological inquiry. But then, in September 1966, Henry I. Louttit, Bishop of South Florida, drew up a formal presentment accusing Pike of heresy and secured the support of others. This presentment was placed before the House of Bishops meeting at Wheeling, West Virginia, October 23–27, 1966. The majority of the bishops present decided against a heresy trial. Such a trial, they believed, would be viewed as a return to a time when the law, both civil and ecclesiastical, "sought to repress and penalize unacceptable opinions." The bishops said, "We believe that our Church is quite capable of carrying the strains of free inquiry and of responsible,

and even irresponsible, attempts to restate great articles of faith
in ways that would speak in positive and kindling terms to men
in our own time." Nevertheless, the majority did proceed to cen-
sure Pike. The bishop, both hurt and infuriated, requested that a
formal investigation be conducted (i.e., a heresy trial).[1]
There ensued considerable debate both in the church press and
in the secular media. Many Episcopalians felt that Bishop Pike
was being persecuted, others that the bishops were remiss in not
conducting a heresy trial. Many felt that Pike was right, while
conceding that he was indiscreet, and charging that the press was
prone to misquote him or quote him out of context. A minority
of the bishops at Wheeling referred to the Anglican Congress
held at Toronto, Canada, in 1963, where new frontiers of mission
were explored:

> We happily agreed that there are frontiers of political and
> technological thought and action confronting Christ's
> Church; and that our mission is to pierce them. Few of us
> have done so, in large part because of the risk involved and
> because of the danger of thè task. Bishop Pike has faced,
> often hurriedly, the demands, intellectual and theological,
> of our time in history, and we commend him for doing so.
> If he has to be a casualty of the Christian mission in our day
> we regret that this is so.[2]

The Pike affair aroused people as it did in part because of the
unsettled conditions of church and society in the 1960s, because
of the visibility of the radical theologians through the mass
media, and because of the furor raising serious questions concerning the church in general and the Episcopal Church in particular. What of its general health? What of its professions of faith,
professions so widely contested in modern America? What of its
liturgy, widely regarded as archaic and out of tune with the
times? What of its composition, largely white, Anglo-Saxon, and
dominated politically by men?

John Knox Addresses the Issues

John Hines, Presiding Bishop of the Episcopal Church at the time of the Wheeling meeting of the House of Bishops, appointed a committee to consider the wider issues emerging out of the debate concerning Bishop Pike. Chaired by Bishop Stephen F. Bayne, Jr., the committee met to draft a report in time for the General Convention of 1967 in Seattle. The committee first asked, "What obligations does the Church have for encouraging theological enquiry and social criticism?" John Knox, an Episcopalian and a New Testament scholar teaching at Union Theological Seminary in New York, was the most influential of the committee consultants. He went right to the heart of the matter and asked, What is the church? He assumed that most thoughtful Christians would acknowledge it to be an identifiable community, created by God for the welfare of humanity. No radical theologian this. The church was created, he believed, through an historical development culminating in Christ by whom it is kept alive into the present. Knox wrote:

> I believe that we would further agree in finding its essential inner being to consist in a shared memory of the Lord Jesus and in a shared experience of the Spirit, apprehended not only as God's Spirit but also as the actual living presence of Christ crucified; and that we should agree also in recognizing that, despite its failures and infidelities, this community of memory and the Spirit is, and has always been, characterized by a distinctive way of life—of thinking, feeling, acting—that is appropriate to, and consequent upon, its nature as the community it is, and which is, therefore, recognizable and inseparably its own.[3]

As such the church should encourage theological inquiry for, as Knox affirmed, participation in the church involves understanding what is being participated in. Not only is it seeing the truths implied in Christian living, but also understanding their relationship to other truths known to the Christian from various sources outside of the church, truths that enhance our experience as participants in Christ. But all such inquiry is encouraged only "so long as the object of it is the fuller understanding and the clearer explication of what is found in the Church's existence."

As to the encouragement of social criticism, Knox explained that rightly understood social criticism proceeds out of the essential character of the church. He wrote:

> The Church's concern about the unjust and inhuman structures of society, insofar as it is authentically its own, belongs to its existence as the particular community it is, and, on that account is *sui generis*. The Church has its own peculiar way of being relevant to the order (or, disorders) of the world. It may not take this way, but there is no other way for it to take and still be relevant *as the Church*. The fuller realization of the Church's own true nature and the fuller discharging of its own mission in the world are really one thing. For the Church is by definition a fellowship in the love of God, and its mission is to be the constantly growing sphere of a constantly deepening reconciliation.[4]

Here was a definition in tune with modern New Testament scholarship, as well as with liturgical and ecumenical studies. "The Church," said Knox, "is by definition a fellowship in the love of God, and its mission is to be the constantly growing sphere of a constantly deepening reconciliation." The church, according to this way of thinking, is an organic body, a people of God. Or, to put it in terms used at Vatican II and in *Lumen Gentium*, the church as the body of Christ is "the sacrament of Christ." Representing him "in the full and ancient meaning of the term, she really makes him present."[5] She does this as she *is* a fellowship in the love of God and as in mission she *is* the constantly growing sphere of a constantly deepening reconciliation.

Building on this definition of the church, Knox said:

Here is the distinctly Christian ground for the abhorring of
all injustice, cruelty, and neglect, whether among individuals or within the structures of our social, economic,
and political existence. In the realized meaning of the
Church, as the body of Christ in which his saving health is
offered to all nations, lies the immediate source of any distinctly Christian contribution to the understanding or solution of ethical issues, individual or social. Not only is it the
obligation of the Church to make this contribution; insofar
as it realizes its true nature it *will* make it.[6]

However, just as the church is not expected to encourage
theological inquiry inconsistent with its true nature, so it is not
expected to encourage social criticism false to its own true nature. Specifically, the church's self-understanding and its social
criticism must arise out of its very existence as a fellowship in
the love of God. It must not arise out of its condition as an institution among institutions subject to the dictates of its secular
environment. It may, nevertheless, be reminded of its true nature
and mission by events in society at large, acknowledging that
God in Christ is often at work in society, beckoning the church
to join in his healing, reconciling work.

To argue thus is to admit that the church can be and often is
apostate. Stephen Bayne, speaking at the General Convention
meeting in Detroit in 1961, criticized the church for being other
than its true self, reflecting as a mirror the society in which it
lived. "Let the church be the church," he cried. Joachim Wach,
an Episcopalian teaching at the University of Chicago, wrote of
the church and of Christianity as a founded religion which began
with a circle of disciples around its Master and became in time
an institution dedicated to the preservation of the memory and
the power of its founder. In time it began to lose sight of its origins
and its mission, devoting more and more of its energies to self-

Small Groups →

preservation and aggrandizement. The situation demanded and inspired reforms in the light of the church's origins in Christ.[7] As the philosopher A.N. Whitehead commented, "The tender vision of Galilean humility was replaced in Christian tradition by the overpowering imagery of Caesar's court."[8] Renewal and reform (*metanoia*) were seen to concern not only individuals but the church itself, the people of God, a fellowship (*koinonia*) in the love of God which too often tends to become a fellowship in self-love. As such the church confirms us in our selfishness and prejudices, asking little and promising much, leading its adherents into the jaws of hell.

There was realized, in the time we are considering, a vital dynamic in the church, a dynamic of decline and renewal, decay and reform, death and rebirth. It is possible to regard the Episcopal Church from 1950 on as a fellowship engaged in Christ's work of reconciliation, while at the same time, and all too often, being an institution among institutions, self-regarding and in need of reform. The church *wås* the church during these years, but it was also less than the church and its own worst enemy, if not all of the time, then time and time again.

From this vantage point it is possible to regard the "radical theologians" as reformers, as well as detractors. They expressed in theological and philosophical terms the sense "that Christianity is primarily mission and service in the world and for the neighbour, and consequently that Christian experience is 'secular,' that is, worldly, political and historical in character."[9] And the new morality, in the form conveyed by Joseph Fletcher in *Situation Ethics*, was intended to call the church back from captivity to complex legalisms to the Gospel rule of love. Christian ethics, said Fletcher, "is not a scheme of living according to a code, but a continuous effort to relate love to a world of relativities through a casuistry obedient to love; its constant task is to work out the strategy and tactics of love for Christ's sake."[10]

Christian ethics, that is, concerns the realization of a fellowship in the love of God and its mission of reconciliation.

Seeking to be a Fellowship: Education and Liturgy

From 1950 on there was considerable activity focused on the more complete realization of the church as a people, a fellowship in the love of God. The church thus sought, whether consciously or not, to be reformed and thus to become more fully that which it was meant to be. As a denomination the Episcopal Church had long suffered the slurs of those who regarded its worship as too formal and its congregations as unfriendly, the church seeming to be more a club for the affluent than a fellowship of forgiven sinners dependent upon one another. Among the indications that there were those seeking to combat the negative image there was the development of Clinical Pastoral Education (CPE), based on the pioneering work of Anton Boisen and Russel Dicks. CPE was designed to assist the clergy of all denominations to discover their own identities as persons, to better understand their pastoral vocations, to integrate theology and the life sciences, to build and maintain healthy interpersonal relationships, and to learn not by reading books but by studying people.[11] In time all Episcopal seminaries encouraged, if they did not require, students to have at least one quarter of CPE. An Episcopal theologian, Albert T. Mollegen, found the interpersonal, relational orientation of CPE conducive to Anglican ecclesiology, to developing biblical theology, and to the teachings of Paul Tillich, whom he had known and assisted in the development of a viable Christology. The most prestigious CPE center, that of St. Elizabeth's Hospital in Washington, D.C., under the leadership of an Episcopalian, Ernest Bruder, was dominated by the Washington School of Psychiatry and the relational teachings of the maverick psychiatrist, Harry Stack Sullivan. Here was strong support for the cultivation in the church of attitudes and skills aimed at creating and sustaining meaningful fellowship, for Sullivan and his pupils aimed at health through healing of broken relationships, that is, in theological terms, through reconciliation. In turn such theologians as Mollegen and his colleague Ruel

CPE - Neg effect

Howe, as well as Tillich, whom they both admired, helped this psychiatric community understand the religious symbols encountered in interpersonal therapies.

The emphasis on CPE in the seminaries also had its negative effects. It promoted, whether it approved or not, a kind of introversion, a greater concern for self-improvement than for service to those in need. Seminarians increasingly sought assistance through analysis and other forms of psychotherapy during the 1950s. CPE equipped clergy with valuable skills, but it also tended to promote an understanding of the pastor as therapist, without providing such training as would validate such an understanding. The clinical model of the ordained professional was not without its dangers, both for the clergy and for their client-parishioners.

As we shall have reason to note later, the clinical/pastoral model of ministry was not without challenges during the 1960s and 70s. As the crises of the times developed, centering upon civil rights and urban riots, anti-war protests and women's liberation, many viewed the ordained minister as social activist/change agent and others concentrated attention on clergy as professionals. However, with the emergence of a new Prayer Book there developed an understanding of ordained ministry in terms of word and sacrament, the priest being viewed by Urban T. Holmes as the "enchanter," "one who mediates the presence of transcendent reality" and "awakens mankind to the revelatory character of their community experience."[12] Still—largely in the context of the professional model of ministry—the clinical/pastoral understanding persisted.

While this venture in the education of the clergy was occurring, church leaders were paying increasing attention to group dynamics, a branch of social psychiatry. The work of Kurt Lewin was developed in this country through the National Training Laboratories, chiefly at Bethel, Maine.[13] In time the National Council of Churches was supporting national training laboratories held annually at Green Lake, Wisconsin. Group dynamics became an important factor in the reform of the church, as clergy and laity availed themselves of training and learned through "T groups" and other methods both how to form and sustain groups and how to pursue desired tasks through such groups. Parish life conferences became commonplace and people were introduced to role-playing, goal-setting, and frank interpersonal encounters. At its best the applications of group techniques to parish life was productive of a greater sense of fellowship, a more realistic management of parish activities, and many instances of genuine reconciliation among previously alienated people. At its worst group dynamics was used to manipulate others, did much damage to sensitive souls not prepared for frank encounters, and contributed to the introversion of the church rather than to a sense of fellowship realized through mission—the mission of reconciliation reaching out in ever widening circles to encompass those beyond the church walls. A great danger was that of the idolization of the group and the too facile identification of the Holy Spirit with a group's spirit.

At the same time a revolution was taking place in Christian education. Randolph Crump Miller, teaching at Yale in the 1950s, decried the secularist influence of "John Dewey and his cohorts," and called for education theory that made use of psychological and sociological insights only as they related to theological understanding. Much in debt to Martin Buber, Miller writing in 1953 located in *relationship* the key educational concept:

> Christian nurture takes place when the believer trusts in God and in turn God's gracious favor comes to him, because that grace was there all the time awaiting the act of faith. Therefore, the application of theology to education leads to a dynamic personal relationship of faith and grace, and the ideas of theology arising from the relationship of men to God are guides to a greater and deeper experience of God.[14]

This perspective was fundamental in the development of the
Seabury Plan, the Episcopal Church's new, costly, exciting,
daunting educational program.
  Begun in 1947, when Presiding Bishop Henry Knox Sherrill
appointed John Heuss as director of the church's Department of
Christian Education, this plan or curriculum had as a premise
the conviction that Christian education concerned not only Sunday schools, but the entire Christian community. Early in Heuss's
work "The Church's Teaching Series" was produced, providing
in readable form fundamental teachings of the church (biblical,
historical, theological, liturgical, ethical and pastoral), forming
bases for adult education and for graded curricular materials.
Using insights from group dynamics and from Paul Tillich's
method of correlation (Ruel Howe's *Man's Need and God's Answer*
owed much to Tillich and was used in the curricular development), the Seabury lesson plans focused attention upon students
as gathered in the classroom. Teachers were expected to resist
mere transmission of content and to assist students in discover-
ing their own ways, together, into the circle of faith. Content was
to be provided as required. There was much discussion in the
church as the graded materials appeared and local congregations
strove to use them in widely varying situations. Some suggested
that while the children being taught might be happier, they were
theologically illiterate; others protested that the plan made ex-
cessive demands on teachers and was designed for use in large
urban/suburban parishes with abundant resources, rather than
small or rural parishes and missions with severely limited
resources. Others protested that the church had sold out to group
dynamics and social psychology in general and the protesters
turned to Presbyterian or Canadian curricula, or else returned to
St. James or Pittsburgh plans. Nevertheless, the introduction of
the Seabury Plan was accompanied by a sharp upswing in Sunday school enrollment, the church was conscious as it had not
been for some time of its educational vocation, and the fellowship of the local church in many places was strengthened.[15]

With Philip Phenix of Columbia University, many church leaders began to see the church's mission in terms of education, in the broad sense of education as involving interpersonal relationships plus content, with content and group dynamics interrelated.[16]

Simultaneously, liturgical revision and renewal was proceeding, moving steadily toward a revision of the Book of Common Prayer. There was much concern, especially among liturgiologists and theologians, that the 1928 Book of Common Prayer had not sufficiently accomplished the principles of its framers. These principles included "enrichment" and "flexibility," citing, among other things, the need for greater variation in liturgical usage in a pluralistic society. A review of the 1928 Prayer Book was conducted and a series of studies published between 1950 and 1963. Then came *The Liturgy of the Lord's Supper* (1967), a trial use, and further studies and trial uses eventuating in a new prayer book, adopted by the General Conventions of 1976 and 1979.[17] Fundamental to this revision was the realization of the basic principles of the liturgical movement on the Continent and in Great Britain. David Edwards accurately identified those principles when writing,

The liturgical movement springs from an insistence on the corporate nature of Christian worship. This is not an obsession with the trivialities of the sanctuary, although it has been accompanied by a keen interest among the more scholarly in the historic forms of worship. At its heart, this is a vision of the People of God assembled around the Word of God. The Word is proclaimed through sermon, scripture and sacrament. The book is opened, the Communion bread is broken, the wine is poured. The people respond by joyful praise and by a conscious dedication, as a fellowship, to their work of service and evangelism in the world.[18]

The emphasis in liturgical revision, informed by the liturgical movement, was on the church as a fellowship in the love of God carrying out its mission (Christ's mission) of reconciliation as its fellowship encompassed more and more people through the work of service and evangelism. In some ways, the movement had the effect of reviving Thomas Cranmer's ideals, evident in the first two books of Common Prayer and in his striving for the realization of communion through word and sacraments, which was for him critical in the realization of the commonweal in Tudor England.[19]

In the parish churches, as the liturgical revision proceeded during the 1960s, there was a shifting away from Morning Prayer to the Eucharist as normative for congregational worship. Family services, often enlivened with folk masses, and with varying degrees of informality, grew in popularity. The laity became more prominently involved in worship, reading the Scripture, leading the intercessions, and administering the cup. New churches were designed to encourage congregational participation. The kiss of peace was introduced and in some places came to be the high point of the liturgy. Attention shifted away from the priest at the altar and the preacher in the pulpit to the fellowship assembled, with the priest as the president or presiding member of the parish family.

The liturgical movement, associated with the names of Odo Casel, Louis Bouyer, Gabriel Hebert, Massey Shepherd, Al Shands, and a host of others, was affecting the church's life to its very core. It was presenting Christianity, in Horton Davies' words, describing Hebert's teaching, "'as a way of life for the worshipping community' which was a corporate renewal of faith (through the theology proclaimed in Sermon and Sacrament), a commitment and consecration (through the Offertory), and an incentive to serve and transform the fragmented society outside, as the very mission of the Church."[20]

Consequently the church was recovering not only the vision of the primitive church but also the vision of Anglican theologians of the sixteenth and seventeenth centuries, of Hooker and Andrewes and many others.[21]

There were those dissatisfied with the effects of the liturgical movement in the Episcopal Church. In addition to those who simply resisted liturgical change (usually resisting all change), there were others, such as the poet W.H. Auden, who objected to the awkward, colloquial, and ineffective language of some of the new texts. There were still others who objected to what they viewed as an over-reliance on liturgies of the early church, such as that of the third-century Hippolytan Church Order, arguing that such liturgies were ill-suited to twentieth-century society. Some found fault with the new family services and the tendency to reduce all worship to the level of three-year olds. Stephen Bayne, for one, especially regretted the demise of the full-bodied sermon in favor of a brief homily suited to all ages. He also faulted the 1967 trial liturgy for neglecting penitence. "I understand and share the contemporary wish to escape from the gloom of the Reformation and post-reformation eucharistic devotion," he said. "A wedding garment is indicated, or a head-anointing and face washing, no doubt. But the man who is to wear the garment still is coming to a banquet which he has no right to share. The communicant who is able to take his place in the offering of the eucharistic sacrifice is simply not worthy of this, if it is the re-enactment by our Lord, in and among us, of His offering which I take it to be."[22] Some were so disturbed that they left the Episcopal Church for one of the several splinter groups then forming. Others remained within the church but allied themselves with The Prayer Book Society, founded to defend the 1928 Prayer Book and its continued use. Nevertheless, in spite of its faults, the liturgical movement in the Episcopal Church fostered a sense of the church as a people, a fellowship, a community, the body of Christ, united in the love of God for the sake of reconciliation in the world.

Liturgical revision did not end with the publication of the new Prayer Book. A new hymnal was approved by General Convention in 1982 and discussion continued concerning the place of confirmation in the life of the church, an issue of critical impor-

tance to everyone involved. The distinction between baptism with water and confirmation—baptism with the Spirit—was declared untenable by the liturgical scholars. We are baptized both by water and the Holy Spirit, and the revisers preferred to eliminate a separate rite of confirmation while making allowance for the renewal of baptismal vows. Not everyone was willing to accept this, although agreeing that the Spirit was given in baptism. The discussion has continued, and perhaps it indicates the necessity of continuing liturgical revision and further trial use. The decade of the 80s has been one in which more and more people have discovered the riches of the new Prayer Book while discussion of the further revision of that book has proceeded.

During the late 70s and into the 80s Christian education has been viewed increasingly in relation to liturgy. Amongst the foremost educators in the Episcopal Church has been John H. Westerhoff, III, who prefers to speak of "catechesis" which is intergenerational and is viewed as a pilgrimage on which all church members go the entirety of their lives. He notes: "With the reform of the Sunday liturgy into a family- oriented, participating, communal celebration of word and sacrament, there is renewed interest in the relationship of learning and liturgy."[23] To avoid the dangers involved in too great a concentration on learning in relation to liturgy, Westerhoff also emphasizes pastoral and moral settings for education, and combines the three in this way:

> The liturgical context best aids us to know the story and vision of the community or to acquire, enhance, and enliven faith; the pastoral setting best aids us to internalize the story and vision of the community or make divine revelation known; and the moral setting best aids us to live the story and vision of the community or realize our vocation.[24]

Furthermore, there is to be seen a relationship between learning and the renewed understanding of initiation in terms of a pilgrimage that lasts all of one's life. The teachings of Piaget, Kohlberg, Gilligan and Fowler on moral development have spurred on concern to develop whole-parish, entire-life catechesis.[25] The changed perspective does not necessarily mean, as Westerhoff suggests, that "Sunday school" will cease to be significant in the future, but there is little doubt that if the catechetical revolution continues this institution with roots in the eighteenth century will change. One indication of change in relation to the new Prayer Book has been the development, beginning in 1976, of the "Living the Good News" curriculum by the Diocese of Colorado, a curriculum now widely in use in the Episcopal Church. This curriculum "brings together families and the church community in shared faith and worship. Using Scriptures appointed in the lectionary, lessons are geared to six age levels—preschool, primary, intermediate, junior high, senior high, and adult—and integrated with eucharistic worship."[26] The focus in the 1980s has been increasingly on the parish as a fellowship, a learning fellowship, a worshipping fellowship, being equipped for mission.

Theodore Wedel, Warden of the College of Preachers, spoke of the problem confronting the church in twentieth-century industrial society, saying that the problem for us (those of the early 60s when he wrote)

consists of recreating within and alongside the church's institutional activities, the Christian community in which Christian charity can bring to men and women the gift of the glorious liberty of the children of God. For if we turn for a vision of what Christian fellowship might be when true to the norm of the New Testament, the wonder and glory of the *koinonia Spiritu Sancti* leaps to life. Here, where "there is neither Jew nor Greek, there is neither slave nor free, there is neither male nor female; for you are all one in Christ Jesus" (Gal. 3:28), exclusion is apostasy. Here is a brotherhood of penitence and gratitude. Here the Spirit power at work is not one engendered in a frail human group trusting in its own ability to free captives of isolation or to bring the gift of human dignity to victims of mass dehumanization, but God himself. Here is a "colony of heaven" in the midst of a dying world, one that enjoys a foretaste of a new heaven and earth beyond mortality's dread end.[27]

The *koinonia Spiritu Sancti* (fellowship of the Holy Spirit) was in process of re-formation during the 1950s, 60s and beyond. CPE and group dynamics, the revision of the church's education program and of its worship, all aimed at the realization of the fellowship, to some degree were imperfect, but all contributed to a livelier sense of fellowship in the Episcopal Church.

The "Ministry of the Laity" and the Church

There was another movement of importance during the years following 1950, one that influenced the church's developing self-understanding. This was identified with the phrase "Ministry of the Laity" and with the activity of the laity in the German Church during World War II, the church behind the Iron Curtain, and with the ecumenical movement, especially the Department of the Laity of the World Council of Churches. Among the numerous books on the subject there were Yves Congar's *Jalons pour une théologie du laicat* (1953), Hendrik Kraemer's *A Theology of the Laity* (1958), a scholarly study by Alden Drew Kelley of Kenyon College, called *The People of God: A Study in the Doctrine of the Laity* (1962), and the popular *The Ministry of the Laity: A Biblical Exposition* (1962) by Francis O. Ayres, founder of Parishfield in Michigan, one of several communities in the United States promoting the ministry of the laity.

The great slogan of the movement was "the laity is the church," usually followed by the assertion that "the church is ministry."[28]

The church was understood to be "the body of Christ," a fellowship "of believing and adoring men and women, but a body none the less," whose ministry is that of reconciliation, defined by John Macquarrie as "activity whereby the disorders of existence are healed, its imbalances redressed, its alienations bridged over."[29] Robert Grant, of the University of Chicago, wrote of "the gospel of reconciliation" (2 Cor. 5:19) in a pre-Lambeth 1978 essay, emphasizing first and foremost reconciliation to God, but noting that the primary reconciliation essentially involves the reconciliation of alienated persons and groups and nations.[30]

The focus was on the laity, the *laos tou theou*, the entire people of God, differentiated after the first beginnings of the church into clergy and laity (non-clergy, plebeians). The damaging development of clericalism early in the church's history was noted by the scholars who stressed the need for a return to the biblical understanding. Macquarrie spoke of the ministry of the church *being* its service. "Christ himself," he wrote in *Principles of Christian Theology* (1966), "was identified with the 'servant of the Lord' of whom we read in deutero-Isaiah. The Church, as continuing the work of Christ in the world, has also the role of a servant, and we can think of the image of the 'servant of the Lord' as one that elucidates the character of the Church."[31]

Kraemer had identified earlier the ministry and thus the church itself with *diakonia* (servanthood), "rooted in the person of Christ." "The church is Diakonia," Kraemer proclaimed. He further argued that all Christians are *diakonoi*, called to minister. He noted the importance of Ephesians 4:11, 12, a passage that emphasizes the oneness and wholeness of the church: "And he gave some to be apostles, some to be prophets, some to be evangelists and some as shepherds and teachers, for the equipment of the saints for the work of diakonia, for the upbuilding of the body of Christ." Kraemer pointed out that it was incorrect to place a comma between "for the equipment of the saints" and "for the work of diakonia" or ministry. Remove the comma and the meaning is radically altered. The removal, Kraemer wrote, restores to the text the meaning which fits in with the picture the New Testament gives of *all* the saints, i.e. all the members, being ministers, servants to the upbuilding of the Church. It rules out the use of the text as a corroboration for the condition of the Church as we know it by tradition, viz. the "ministry," the diakonia as a specialized sphere. Of this specialized sphere the Church in its primitive, fluid state was scarcely conscious. All the stress was on the diakonia, the ministry of the whole membership, because the Church as a whole stood under the same token as its Lord, i.e. "servant- ship."[32]

Professor Kelley, reviewing the Biblical evidence, concluded that "the church in its aspects of nature and mission is an indivisible whole and should be regarded as that." He went on to say, "The church understood as the People of God is for the world in what it is and what it does. Accordingly, the laity is to be defined theologically by defining the church; not by contrast to the church regarded as clerics and monastics, nor as *part* of the church, nor as an *order* of the church. The laity *is* the church, period."[33]

In a book of essays published in 1963, J.A.T. Robinson expressed the revolutionary character of this rethinking of the church by asserting "the clergy are *the servants* of the laity," citing Hans Reudi Weber as saying, "The laity are not helpers of the clergy so that the clergy can do their job, but the clergy are helpers of the whole people of God, so that the laity can be the Church." This point of view is not, Bishop Robinson believed, detrimental to the clergy. Rather, as the ministry of the laity is realized there is "a tremendous increase and release of their (the clergy's) ministry, as they discover themselves for the first time as the servants of the servants of God." He believed that this understanding, which was also a medieval papal understanding in a limited sense, is "the clue to the whole revolution. For we can never hold too high a doctrine of the ordained ministry if we really see it, as the New Testament does, as the ministry of the servant, in direct extension of the ministry of the Son of Man who came not to be ministered unto but to minister."[34]

Fran Ayres rightly recognized the difficulties this movement faced. Writing in 1962 he said:

> Fifteen years after the war, the ministry of the laity is widely acclaimed. Convention addresses, pamphlets, articles on the present state of the church, sermons calling for advance, special conferences—all have urged a development of the ministry of the laity. In the United States it has become a slogan of our time, one's enthusiasm for the concept is a test of one's openness and mobility.
>
> But with what a radically different meaning! The layman remains a second-class citizen, an assistant to the clergy, primarily a maintenance man in the institutional church.... The church as a whole has remained unmoved.[35]

Ayres then asserted the obvious, "The church urgently needs renewal."[36]

The frustration has continued into the 1980s, although there was more organized effort made through the national organization of the Episcopal Church and through such agencies as the Alban Institute and the Audenshaw Foundation. Also there has been strong lay participation in such renewal efforts as the Cursillo movement and Faith Alive—sometimes to the alarm of the clergy. Cynthia Wedel, as one of the six presidents of the World Council of Churches, spoke of the sixth assembly of the World Council of Churches in Vancouver, Canada, saying that the clergy, by numbers and distinctive dress, would be most visible. But, she said, there would be hundreds of lay persons there.

If Vancouver 1983 is to speak to and for the church, the laity who are present will be the key to making such speaking effective.

It is valuable, of course, for professional theologians and
church leaders to discuss doctrine and church order and
other issues in the life of the churches. But if the Church of
Jesus Christ has a message and a mission to our frightened
and strife-torn world, it is the great army of lay Christians
who must embody that witness in their life and work.[37]

There were many who heeded her call and others who did not
hear at all.

Increasingly renewal was perceived as related to the rethinking of the ordained ministry. Kelley rightly pointed out that "the
problem of the laity" was in truth "the problem of the clergy."
He went on to say, "that if there be any solution, the finding of it
will be partly the responsibility of the ordained ministry who usually function in the church as channels of authority."[38] R o b -
inson saw the solution as involving a change in perception, a
renunciation of the picture of "a struggling vicar grappling with
an impossible task, visiting, organizing, evangelizing, preaching,
praying, teaching, celebrating, while his churchwardens, and
those of the faithful who can be persuaded, help him."[39] " T h e
whole Church, ordained and unordained alike, is called to be a
lay body," wrote the Bishop of Woolwich. "By this of course I do
not mean…that it is not to have its sacramental ministers, but
that it is essentially and always a body which is immersed in the
world."[40]

There was considerable discussion in these years of the ministry and of alternatives to the customary three-fold ordained
ministry of the church. In Alaska, and elsewhere, the principles
of Roland Allen were being followed through the establishment
of indigenous clergy of various categories. The non-stipendiary
ministry was discussed also, and in some places the worker-
priest concept was tried with varying degrees of success and
failure. In time the diaconate was revived with the establishment,
to a degree after the Roman Catholic model, of what was some-

times called the "permanent diaconate," to distinguish it from the transitional diaconate of those called to the order of priests. For the Episcopal Church the main development in this revival of the diaconate still lies ahead. The episcopate was receiving considerable attention, with special attention given at Lambeth 1978 and beyond, with concern expressed as bishops shouldered increasing administrative and financial responsibilities. The presbyterate was regarded by many as the order most in need of scrutiny and reform, especially as in a national survey parish priests declared that most of their time was consumed in administration, the task they liked least and for which they felt most unprepared.

The report of the special committee to the House of Bishops "On the Ordination of Women" in 1972 reflected much serious thought on the threefold ordained ministry and pointed the way in which much future discussion would go. The diaconate was seen as seriously in need of attention, contemporary understanding being "murky and confused." Some viewed it as no more than a stepping-stone to the priesthood, others as barely distinguishable from the ministry of a lay person. The report suggested:

> If the ordained diaconate is not merely a vestigial historical fragment, or an apprenticeship, it seems clearly to be a ministry of service. It may be distinguished from the service to which all Christians are called simply by intensity and by the authority and accountability conveyed in ordination, of which perhaps the liturgical privilege of reading the Gospel is a token.

The question was asked, "Should the diaconate be seen as primarily a work of advocacy of the poor, the sick, the dispossessed?"[41] We may be able to see here a suggestion that the renewed diaconate could be an effective symbol of the service ministry of the whole people of God, modeling that ministry but

also providing leadership in it, representing Christ the Servant
to the world and making the fellowship in the love of God more
visible and more responsive to the needs of others.

The renewal of the diaconate was spurred on by a study commissioned by the House of Bishops in 1977, issuing in the report
The Church, the Diaconate, and the Future presented to the House
of Bishops at the 1979 General Convention in Denver. From that
point on the development of diaconal ministry, both through the
order of deacons and in the service ministry of the entire church,
proceeded, aided by the National Center for the Diaconate in
Boston and by a growing number of conferences and publications on the subject.[42]

The 1972 report to the House of Bishops spoke of priesthood
with reverence, acknowledging that the New Testament knows
of only one priest, the Lord. It said:

> The "Royal Priesthood" of 1 Peter 2:9 is derivative from
> Christ's High Priesthood—it refers to the ministry of loving
> service which all Christians share because of their in-
> clusion, through baptism, in His Priestly Body. The word
> "priest" as applied to individual ministers seems not to
> have found its way into the Church's vocabulary until the
> end of the second century. Any developed doctrine of min-
> isterial priesthood is still slower to appear; indeed it may
> be said that the Church, in our time, is still unfolding the
> truths about the ministry of the ordained and the un-or-
> dained alike hidden in the mystery of priesthood.[43]

Those ordained to be priests, it was argued, participate in both
Christ's High Priesthood and the Royal Priesthood of all baptized Christians, partaking of both and expressing both in their
ministries. There is also a sense in which ordained priests are in-
strumentally involved in that reconciliation which is mediated
down through the years in and through the church, with all
members sharing in that mediation. "By ordination," the report

" " OF " "

said, "certain members of the Body are called of God and authorized by the Body to speak and act for the High Priest toward the Church and the world. They also speak and act for the Church and the world in making offering for them, through the Son, to the Father." But the priest is not above the *laos* or against it. The priest "is rather within the *laos* as a particular focus or symbol or effective means of Christ's action toward the Church and the world, and of the Church's thankful response, through Christ, to the Father."[44]

The episcopate was also viewed in the report to the House of Bishops as "marked by the mystery of representation." The report went on to say:

> All that has been said of priesthood applies to the bishop, of course. What is added is his peculiar ministry of continuity, of unity, of wholeness, of oversight. This ministry, shared with the clergy and laity, and fully collegial, is an incarnation of Christ's actions and qualities. The bishop represents the Lord to His Body and the world. That is to say, it is the eternity of the Son which is the continuity mediated through ordination; it is the complex unity of the person of Jesus Christ—a unity of disciplined, single-minded obedience to mission—which is the source of the unity of the Church; it is the health and wholeness of the Incarnate Lord which is given in the whole state of His Church; it is Christ's compassionate and vigilant care which is mediated in the ministry of the overseer and the pastor. And in all of this, the bishop represents the Church and the world before the Father, in and through the Son.[45]

As with the diaconate and the presbyterate (or priesthood), at heart the ministry is Christ's and through Christ belongs to the church, with the ordained ministers representing both Christ and the church to one another and to the world, effective symbols of the church's ministry, which is Christ's ministry. The report did not go as far in expressing the symbolic nature of the ordained offices of the church as some might have wished and as some were to go in the coming years. But the statements pointed toward a conclusion such as that of Bishop Frensdorff, who argued that "The ordained offices have the quality of a sign [and are thus sacramental] because they express the Church's sacramentality—outward and visible sign of inward and spiritual grace."[46]

James Pike and Norman Pittenger in the Church's Teaching Series volume entitled *The Faith of the Church* (1951) affirmed that the people of God share by grace in Christ's priesthood, have direct access through Christ to God, and are priests to their brothers and sisters because they share Christ's priesthood. They said:

> It is against this background that we must understand the ordained ministry, since its particular task in the Body of Christ is to represent and function for the whole Body in its several responsibilities. A deacon, priest, or bishop is not separated from the Church or its lay members by some impassable gulf. He is the agent of Christ, in His Church, to perform those special functions which are necessary both for the continuation of the Church's life and the fulfillment of what is the task of the whole fellowship.[47]

There were reasons for the frustration of the ministry of the laity to which Ayres referred. The literature concerning this ministry, as well as the concrete experimentation for its realization, were swamped by the events of the 60s and 70s. The crises of the times resulted in some places in an increased clericalism, whether as the result of opposition arising between clergy and laity concerning such matters as Prayer Book revision and women's ordination, or as a result of the necessity, as clergy perceived it, to respond to social strife and societal change in ways that most laity found difficult or objectionable. A gap widened between clerical leadership and the average member of the *laos.* There was also an erosion of clerical authority and an increase of uncertainty among the clergy when dealing with explosive issues. This might have provided a setting for rethinking the nature of the church on the local level had not so many of the laity been divided and confused at the same time. They looked to their clergy for guidance but protested that there was no guidance or that what guidance there was was ill-founded.

Another difficulty involved the application of intellectual understandings to institutional problems, ideals to complex systems. It was clear to some that to take seriously the church as the *laos tou theou* would necessitate institutional adjustments of some magnitude, and before the ministry of the laity could gain substantial ground the ministry of the threefold ordained ministry would have to be rethought. The fact was that such a matter as the ministry of the laity and a theology of the laity could not be achieved without reference to fundamental doctrine. Yves Congar believed that such a task

> is not just a matter of adding a paragraph or a chapter to an ecclesiological exposition which from beginning to end ignores the principles on which a "laicology" really depends. ...At bottom, there can be only one sound and sufficient theology of the laity, and that is a "total ecclesiology."[48]

A Significant Shift in the 80s

In the 1980s attention has shifted from consideration of the threefold order of ministers to the fundamental *order* of the church, which is to say from organization and externals to a focus on the identity of the church. Richard Norris, Episcopal priest and theologian teaching at Union Seminary, New York, a key participant in the Trinity Institute consultation on a theology of priesthood in 1982, contributed to this shifting, focusing attention on "the ministry of word and sacrament." He writes

three fold orders of ministers → order of the church

that the fundamental media of the Church's identity are its characteristic institutions or liturgies, and that what is called "the ministry" represents just one of several interrelated factors which figure in the occurrence or performance of these institutions. The ordained ministry serves and guarantees the identity of the Church only as it ministers to the message which is the burden of the Scriptures and to the life—the life in Christ—which the sacraments, with the Scriptures, communicate. It is the organic complex of ministry, word, and sacrament that orders the Church and is the effective sign of its identity and continuity.[49]

With this understanding the threefold ministry, its "shape and nomenclature," is "of secondary importance." "The threefold ministry is not a priori and of necessity the sole legitimate shape of an ecclesial ministry. What is a priori and of necessity, and what can reasonably be shown never to have been lacking in the Church in one form or another, is precisely a ministry of word and sacrament."[50]

Such reasoning involves consideration of the church as the *laos tou theou*, the entire people of God, whose identity is formed through the ministry of word and sacrament. Its ministry is symbolized and enabled in and through ordained officers of the church, the servants of the church, whose members are ordained for ministry through baptism.[51] This then suggests the image of ordained officers of the church as ministers of word and sacrament, persons "set apart" in and of the church, to nourish the people of God "in discipleship—the business, that is, of growing into Christ in the various callings, responsibilities, and circumstances of human life."[52] These ordained persons serve the church most fully and effectually when they are at work preaching the word and administering the sacraments. It is in relation to this basic understanding that ordained persons serve also, and secondarily, as overseers, pastors, professionals, change-agents, and so on and on. So proceeds a line of thought increasingly explored in the age of the 1979 Prayer Book.

The Crisis in Theological Education

From the 1950s on the Episcopal Church experienced considerable unrest concerning theological education and its seminaries. On behalf of the American Association of Theological Schools, Charles R. Feilding produced a report called *Education for Ministry* (1966) which concluded that "the greater part of the whole theological enterprise seems to be off on a vast archeological dig, preoccupied with the long ago and largely oblivious to the purpose of the expedition."[53]

For the Episcopal Church a Special Committee on Theological Education, chaired by Nathan M. Pusey, president of Harvard, submitted a report to the Seattle General Convention in 1967, called *Ministry for Tomorrow*, prepared by Charles L. Taylor. The report reflected a widespread concern that theological education as pursued in the Episcopal Church's eleven accredited seminaries was too fragmented, too little concerned with the church's mission in contemporary society, and too expensive—largely because of the inefficiency involved in a system of seminaries independent of the church's official governance. It was widely felt that there were too many seminaries for a church the size of the Episcopal Church. The report was prepared "to stimulate improvement in theological education, particularly in the Episcopal Church."[54]

Having debated whether theological education should be designed to produce ministers for the church or specialized theological scholars, or both, the report concluded that "the *professional preparation for ministry* is the primary purpose of seminary education." It then asked what kind of education would best suit such a purpose and answered:

Between a merely practical training and a highly theoretical indoctrination, we believe there is another and better

way—an organic education the focal point of which is the
service to be performed by the minister. That service is
God's mission entrusted to His people—the understanding and spread of the Gospel both in life and word.
Preparation for it therefore means preparation of the person, and will include both his spiritual development for
that service—in that misson, in that life—and his development in intellectual power and knowledge necessary for
the task.[55]

The committee therefore emphasized the education of
generalists rather than specialists, and suggested that "the equipment of the man or woman of God for *the general work of minister-
ing* should be the primary purpose underlying the selection of
persons for the faculty, the buying of books, the subject matter of
the curriculum, the arrangement of the calendar, and everything
else in the life of the seminary."[56]

In addition, the report spoke of the necessity of assisting the
student to develop personal resources, to be sensitive to and able
to address the doubts and confusions arising for all people in the
modern world. This required a "constant interaction between
theory and practice." It argued that the proper setting for the
kind of education envisioned was "*an urban center, near a university, in ecumenical relations with other seminaries.*"[57] Saskatoon

In the end the Pusey-Taylor report called for a Board for
Theological Education to aid seminaries in coping with the challenges, financial and other, facing them. Such a board was
created and set about addressing the crisis in the seminaries. At
one time it recommended a reduction in the number of seminaries, taking into account such matters addressed in the report
as the desirability of an urban setting, in ecumenical relationship
to other seminaries, and benefiting from the resources of major
universities.

The efforts were not altogether successful, but three seminaries—the Episcopal Theological School, the Philadelphia

TASK #I

Divinity School, and the General Theological Seminary—did respond by creating the Episcopal Consortium for Theological Education in the North East (ECTENE) for mutual cooperation. Its major effect was the merger of the Episcopal Theological School and the Philadelphia Divinity School to form the Episcopal Divinity School in Cambridge, Massachusetts, in 1974. Thus the total number of Episcopal seminaries was reduced by one (to be offset by the founding of a new, evangelical seminary in western Pennsylvania, Trinity School for Ministry). From the beginning the Board for Theological Education sought for more responsible ways of dealing with seminary fiscal problems, a labor which was to continue until 1982. The General Convention at New Orleans approved the assessment (variously regarded and treated) of one percent of net disposable income from every parish and mission for theological education in and through the seminaries, resulting in a closer relationship between seminaries and the dioceses of the church.

Another result was to be the institution of a General Ordination Examination (GOE). The 1970 meeting of the House of Bishops at General Convention in Houston, Texas created the General Board of Examining Chaplains, which was required by canon law (Title III.7) to prepare an examination in the areas listed in Canon III.5. The board, chaired by Stephen Bayne, with Charles Long as vice-chairman, studied general examinations in the Church of England and the United Presbyterian Church, U.S.A., and concluded that the seminaries were best equipped to judge the academic competence of their students, while the bishops and their advisors evaluated the personal formation and suitability of candidates for ministry. They then noted:

> A third area related to, but not coincident with those previously mentioned, involves an individual's ability to focus his faith and learning in a way responsive to the needs and demands of people in the world. It is the purpose of these general examinations to offer to the Church a

partial means of assessing a candidate's capability to make this synthesis.[58]

After much work toward a first examination, to be administered in 1972, the board concluded that in the examination the canonical areas (Bible, church history, theology, pastoral care, ethics, contemporary society, liturgics) were to be linked in comprehensive ways. Thus it could measure "a candidate's understanding of the interrelationship of various academic disciplines and his ability to relate such knowledge to professional practice."[59]

The GOE made an impact on theological education, although that impact is not easily assessed. With questions structured in relation to concrete (although most often hypothetical) situations, calling for the application of academic learning in the classical fields, the student was tested as to his or her ability to apply formal learning to pastoral and other situations. Teaching in some of the seminaries began to reflect this methodology, as, for instance, in the use of the case method in the teaching of theology by Owen Thomas at the Episcopal Theological School. The seminaries were also being challenged to assist their students in becoming, not seminary teachers, but professional ministers. The emphasis, as in much else during those years, was on ministry as service enabling the ministry and mission of the entire church.

There were adverse reactions to what was perceived by some scholars as an unwarranted intrusion into the domain of the theological seminaries, a threat to their necessary independence, even to their academic freedom, and an attempt to shut down some of the seminaries with a consequent loss of teaching positions. The GOE was faulted for ignoring content knowledge, for less than adequate evaluation, and for situation questions that were contrived and to a degree false. The GOE was to change in the coming years, but it seemed from the beginning to be in line with the church's agenda—at least in the judgment of some. As to the problem of overcoming the fragmentation of theology as taught in the seminaries—this issue, of concern to all seminaries and not just those of the Episcopal Church, was to remain of major concern, studied in the 1980s by the Association of Theological Schools and the Lilly Endowment.

The imagination of many church leaders was captured by Edward Farley of Vanderbilt University when, in a book related to the Lilly Endowment exploration of theological education, he attacked theological education in the United States. Theology, he claimed, was treated as one discipline among others, a mere part of the four-fold curriculum of biblical, historical, practical, and theological studies, rather than acknowledged for what it is: "a state and disposition of the soul which has the character of knowledge." He attacked the fragmentation of the curriculum, the specialization of the teachers, and the way in which students were unfairly burdened with the task of integration. Theology is grounded in "belief-ful knowing." "Faith describes the way in which the human being lives in and toward God and the world under the impact of redemption." Theology concerns "what happens to that insightfulness when it becomes self-conscious, when it subjects itself to deliberate processes of reflection and inquiry." The result is understanding, or *theologia*. Thus understood, theology is the occupation of the people composing the community of faith—all the people. The clergy are facilitators: "The Church leader, lay or ordained, works to enable the church's ministries and the theological understanding(s) which they require." Primarily they are facilitators of the *theologia* (understanding) essential to the being and activity of the community of faith. Theological seminaries must be first and foremost engaged in equipping persons as facilitators of *theologia* in the community of faith.[60]

Such a goal, if it is to be realized, requires, so it seems to me, a curriculum with one subject, theology, which involves the traditional emphases, taught by persons who would all be professors of theology—not narrow specialists, as they are today. Beyond that, Farley's critique suggests that in order to reform theological education it may be necessary to abandon seminaries as we know them, replacing them with theological institutes designed for the theological education of the entire community of faith, equipping facilitators both lay and clerical. Such institutes would of necessity be staffed by educators whose fundamental committment was to *theologia* (in the broad, inclusive sense of that term) and not to some particular discipline or sub-discipline. The curriculum would be fashioned in relation to the community of faith, with that community providing the operative paradigm, rather than the presently predominant clerical paradigm that seems to rule the seminaries, even when they have lay students. It is to such thoughts, and many others, that the church in the 1980s is being compelled.

The Church Reaches Out

Thus was the church internally occupied with reform and renewal. There were many ways in which this took place; we have looked at but a few. The danger, widely recognized at the time, was that in such self-concern the church would lose sight of its mission, and furthermore, tend to ignore Christ already at work outside the church, beckoning people to join in the work of reconciliation there. But it was the conviction of those who thought, as did John Knox, that in realizing its essential nature as a fellowship in the love of God, the church would be engaged in reconciling activities beyond the immediate fellowship. In addition, it should be noted that in a very real way the church was already a part of secular society, its members in need of reconciling love and forgiveness as they lived, day by day, in the world. One can go on to say that the church is in fact that portion of the world that has fellowship in the love of God and is graced by the reconciling work of Christ.

However, the times were such that the Episcopal Church could no longer spend its energies internally without being challenged by highly charged events in society, events that challenged its existence as a fellowship in the love of God and its commitment to Christ's mission of reconciliation. One image stands out, in the midst of social dissolution and revolutionary violence. That is of John Hines, Presiding Bishop, late in the summer of 1967, reacting to the rioting then ravaging American cities, sensitive to the growing crisis in the nation, the anti-Vietnam demonstrations, and the ferment over civil rights. Hines visited the Bedford-Stuyvesant area of New York City and the slums of Detroit. He then went on to Seattle where, at the opening service of General Convention he preached a sermon that deserves to be regarded as a primary document of the era.[61]

Hines spoke of the despair of those in urban ghettos, despair at ever realizing justice for Black people as long as white people were the administrators of justice. He spoke of a growing conviction that relief for those oppressed would come only through the seizure of power, seizure that would enable Blacks to control their own destinies. He reminded us of the Black, poverty-stricken inhabitants of our cities who wrote off "the Churches as possible allies in their quest for justice, for they have seen little concrete evidence that Church people are concerned about their plight or will take the necessary risk to help redeem it."

What was to be done? Hines had consulted many people, including Black leaders, and challenged the convention to develop a program aimed at empowering the people of the ghettos, encouraging "the use of political and economic power to support justice and self-determination for all men." Here was a critical moment in which the Episcopal Church was confronted with the need to make decisions that would affect its life for years to come. What would the church decide? How would the decisions be made? On the basis of social, political, economic convictions, or on the basis of that understanding of the church as a fellowship in the love of God, dedicated to being the constantly growing sphere of a constantly deepening reconciliation, or—as was more likely—some combination of the two, with the tensions involved causing both pain and joy, disaffection and growth?

Chapter 2

The Episcopal Church and American Society

The Spirit of the Age

The Episcopal Church exists in a post-Christian era. There are still churches being built, multitudes attend church regularly, and societal values still reflect the influence of Christian morals, but the prevalent spirit of the age is no longer Christian, or Judeo-Christian, or even theistic. The spirit of the era from 1950 onward was formed by scientific materialism and social Darwinism, by behaviorism in psychology and logical positivism in philosophy. Empirical verification was considered essential to the acceptance of anything as true, good, or beautiful. Reflecting this spirit and adding new dimensions to it was the developing socio-technical constitution, an innovation threatening the aging political constitution. The socio-technical constitution regarded entrepreneurs and managers as its forefathers, the creators of vast socio-technical systems devoid of political wisdom, concerned, as Langdon Winner has said, "with such matters as the quest for profits, organizational control, and the pleasures of innovation. They have seldom been interested in the significance of their work on the overall structure of society or its justice."[1]

Instead of the ten commandments, the socio-technical constitution recognizes one law, that of "efficiency." So long as the socio-technical systems do not result in catastrophe and are efficient, they are beyond criticism—they are as gods commanding obeisance.

The spirit of the age reflects a shift in America from a production-oriented economy to a service economy. By the 1970s research, education, and government, basic to a service economy, accounted for one half of the Gross National Product. The profile of the work-force dramatically changed, with white-collar workers outnumbering blue-collar workers five to four. Highly skilled technicians, such as engineers and computer programmers, were increasingly in demand; unskilled workers swelled the growing numbers of Americans living below the poverty-line, their jobs eliminated by automation, by changing demands in a constantly shifting economy, and by a host of other developments beyond their control.

The benefits of the new technologies were many and often dramatic; the costs were often very high. Economic prosperity, population growth, the movement of the middle class toward suburbia, and the rapid growth of consumerism were all mixed blessings. The quest for consumer goods and services escalated during this period. In the 1950s the labor force came to be regarded not only as a key element in production, but as a major factor in the growth of the consumption needed to maintain a high level of production. More and more Americans satisfied at least some of their entertainment needs through visits to shopping malls and in the purchase of electronic and other devices to improve the efficiency of their lives and to increase personal pleasure. Advertising flourished and, as the economist John Kenneth Galbraith remarked, the American economy depended on producers who provided products advertised by themselves as essential. In addition, mass media came into its own, as Richard Schickel has pointed out in frightening detail.[2] Television developed into a major influence in American life; Americans spent, by the early 1980s, an average of seven hours a day watching it.

All these observations are simply an indication of the revolutionary nature of the times. More could be said about the development of nuclear power, the sexual revolution, and many other trends. The point here is to note that the spirit of the age was no longer Christian, or theistic, but was focused upon the present, the life abundant, life ever more efficient and pleasurable. The spirit was that of scientific materialism and social Darwinism, whose law was efficiency and whose way of life was expressed in ever-burgeoning consumption for personal gratification.

The American churches were deeply involved in the spirit of the age. Gibson Winter revealed as much in his book *The Suburban Captivity of the Churches* (1960), in which he said, "In place of the sacraments, we have community meetings. In place of the confession, the bazaar; ...in place of community, a collection of functions; ...every church activity seems to lead further into a maze of superficiality which is stultifying the middle class community." Lionel Trilling commented, "Religion nowadays has the appearance of what the ideal modern house has been called, a machine for living." William Chafe, writing about the church in the 50s, reports:

> Instead of creating a community based on faith in God ...the suburban church preached the gospel of comfort and security.... People might say they believed in God, MIT philosopher Houston Smith has said, "but on examination it turns out that many people believe in believing in Him." The church has lost its core, these critics believed, becoming one more manifestation of consumerism. "On weekdays one shops for food... and on Sundays one shops for the Holy Ghost."[3]

Other observers have pointed out that religion in America, where a majority of people claim to believe in God, has tended to become increasingly more privatized, individualized, a matter of personal concern, each individual fashioning out of the options available "a system of sacred values and meanings in keeping with personal needs and preferences. Such privatized religion," says William Clark Roof, "knows little of communal support, and exists by and large independent of institutionalized religious forms."[4]

The situation pointed to a crisis in the life of the church, its susceptibility to cultural influence, its understanding or misunderstanding of itself, and its sense of mission or lack thereof. Here was an implicit challenge to reform and renew the church as a fellowship in the love of God on mission to a society which was increasingly alienated from the Judeo-Christian tradition.

The Black Church

Episcopalians were jolted out of their complacency in the 1960s by the civil rights movement, by growing resistance to American involvement in Southeast Asia, and by movements for the liberation of women and Native Americans, all of which challenged Americans in general. Young Episcopalians joined the youth of other groups in protesting that American leaders were betraying the American creed of equality, liberty, and the rule of law bequeathed by Washington, Jefferson, Madison, and the other founders of the nation. Samuel Huntington has written of the Harvard Commencement of 1969 at which Meldon Levine delivered the English Oration, protesting:

We are not...conspiring to destroy America. We are attempting to do the reverse; we are affirming the values which you [our parents and our teachers] have instilled in us.... You have told us repeatedly that trust and courage were standards to emulate. You have convinced us that equality and justice were inviolable concepts. You have

taught us that authority should be guided by reason and tempered by fairness. *And we have taken you seriously.*[5]
    In various ways Episcopalians were discovering that Christians dedicated to reconciliation were contributing directly or indirectly to the oppression of a racial minority and to the waging of a brutal war. The challenge to the Episcopal Church came from those who in imperfect ways, sometimes unjust ways, were recalling the church in its essential being as a fellowship in the love of God to its mission of reconciliation, rather than oppression and destruction. They had been evangelized and so were impatient with anything short of total dedication to Gospel principles. Idealistic, naive, even simplistic and unfair, many represented the stuff of which heroes are made.
    Here was one basis for the developing ferment in the land. Another was the transition I have mentioned from an industrial to a socio-technical society. Consider, for instance, the migration in the early 40s of two million Black people from the rural south to the northern, mid-western, and western industrial centers, providing manual labor in defense-related factories. The status quo was shaken: relocated Black people demanded equal pay and equal rights, white workers rebelled, bloody riots broke out in Detroit, harbingers of greater violence to come.[6] This was the beginning. The discontent of the Blacks was exacerbated as heavy industry was replaced by high-technology and manual labor was less in demand. Blacks were the chief victims of this transition, largely because of poorer education and the prejudice of whites. Many Blacks lacked the special skills required by the new technology.
    The civil rights movement of the 1950s logically focused on education (Brown versus the Board of Education, for instance) and was concerned with discrimination in general. A critical moment came in Montgomery, Alabama, in 1955, when a highly respected Black member of the community, Rosa Parks, riding a bus refused to give up her seat to a white person, as law and custom required. She inspired a tide of non-violent resistance.

The Episcopal Church was forced by the course of events to recognize the existence of deep-seated racial prejudice in its midst. The great Black leader, W.E.B. Dubois, had said in 1903 that the Episcopal Church had "probably done less for black people than any other aggregation of Christians." The extent to which this was true was directly related to racial prejudice, expressed and unexpressed. Prejudice had been openly expressed in what Robert A. Bennett has described as "the 'southern strategy' of segregation without representation," and covertly in a national strategy to prevent black Episcopalians from full participation in the power structures of the church.[7] In the 1970s Black Episcopalians constituted a small minority of total church membership (about 3.5%), due in part to discrimination. There had been Black suffragan bishops as well as bishops of missionary districts such as Haiti and Liberia. It was not until 1970 that there was a Black diocesan bishop, John Burgess of Massachusetts. There had been recently a Black vice president of the House of Deputies, Charles Willie, but the first president did not come until the election in 1979 of Charles R. Lawrence.

To realize its true nature as a fellowship in the love of God, dedicated to reconciliation, the Episcopal Church moved to eradicate racial prejudice. Robert Bennett, writing in 1974, spoke of three developments that inspired hope.[8] First was the increase in numerical strength caused by the immigration in the first half of the twentieth century of Black Anglicans from places such as the West Indies. Second was the impact of the civil rights movement, which encouraged Black solidarity and made Episcopalians in general more receptive to the hopes and dreams of Black Americans. This receptivity was "evident in the formation of the interracial action group known as the Episcopal Society for Cultural and Racial Unity (ESCRU), and in the establishment of the General Convention Special Program (GCSP) in 1967 to meet the needs of Black determination." Third was the emergence of a Black caucus, "the Union of Black Episcopalians (UBE) in 1968 providing a forum and lobby for Black interests in the

Church." One important result was the founding in 1972 of the
Absalom Jones Theological Institute as the Episcopal Church's
part in the Interdenominational Theological Center in Atlanta,
Georgia.

Racial prejudice was not eliminated from the Episcopal
Church in the years beginning in 1950, but it was diminished and
the slow process toward integration was begun. There were great
symbolic acts: the election of John Burgess as Bishop of Massachusetts; and the election of Charles Willie and Charles
Lawrence to positions of power in General Convention; the
rebuilding of destroyed Black churches in Mississippi; Black and
white Episcopalians marching together from Selma to
Montgomery; sit-ins resulting in the jailing of such persons as
Mary Peabody and Esther Burgess, the wives of Bishops
Peabody and Burgess, the one white, the other Black; and the
development of the Joint Urban Program, designed to minister
to the needs of the urban poor, chiefly Blacks and Hispanics.

A severe testing came as Black leaders felt the civil rights
movement bogging down, oppression resurgent, and Black
people crying out in rage, turning from non-violence to rioting,
burning and looting. It was in the conflagration of 1966 that the
slogan "Black Power" was born. Stokely Carmichael spoke for
many when he declared that this nation "does not function by
morality, love, and non-violence.... [It functions] by power."[9]

Paralleling the emergence of "Black Power" was the development of "Black Theology." An early proponent of the latter was
Nathan Wright, an Episcopal priest and author of *Black Power and
Urban Unrest* (1967). Wright related Black Power to a theological
understanding of creation:

A God of power, of majesty and of might, who has made
[people] to be in his own image and likeness, must will that
his creation reflect in the immediacies of life his power, his
majesty, and his might. Black power raises, for the healing

of humanity and for the renewal of a commitment to the creative religious purpose of growth, the far-too-long over-looked need for power, if life is to become in the mind of its Creator [what] it is destined to be.[10]

Black Power as Black Theology centered upon liberation, as the statement of the National Committee of Black Churchmen on "Black Theology," issued in June of 1969, indicated:

Black theology is a theology of black liberation. It seeks to plumb the black condition in the light of God's revelation in Jesus Christ, so that the black community can see that the gospel is commensurate with the achievement of black humanity. Black theology is a theology of "blackness." It is the affirmation of black humanity that emancipates black people from white racism, thus providing authentic freedom for both white and black people.... The message of liberation is the revelation of God as revealed in the in-carnation of Jesus Christ. Freedom *is* the gospel. Jesus is the Liberator.[11]

Warner Traynham, an Episcopal priest and able proponent of Black Theology, wrote in 1973 of the church's vocation as the rep-resentative of the Liberator for the liberation of the oppressed. He spoke of the church as the body of Christ, in "the old Anglican formula... 'the extension of the Incarnation'." As such its work is the work of Christ, the work of liberation grounded on hope. He said:

If the Church hopes, she will act on that hope and some-where groans will cease, health will return, the crushed will stand upright as a result. That is why we can say that, where men are liberated, there is God, and the instrument of that liberation is his Church, however it may understand itself, for it does his work in the world.[12]

Black Power and Black Theology challenged the churches.
How did the Episcopal Church react?

The General Convention Special Program, inspired by John
Hines in his opening sermon at Seattle in 1967, was a positive
response to the challenge. After Seattle the Episcopal Church
rearranged its priorities to provide money and leadership for the
program, and a Special Screening and Review Committee was
established to decide which specific enablement projects should
receive money, including in its considerations enablement for
Native Americans and Hispanics as well as Blacks. Fundamental to the program was the conviction that, once given, the money
was no longer controlled by the church. This was seen as necessary if *Black* power was to be realized. It meant taking risks. Many
Episcopalians objected to some or all of the grants made, viewing the program with alarm and the recipients as anarchists or
worse.[13] Some parishes, and then some dioceses, began to withhold funds that might find their way into the General Convention Special Program. As a result the church as the fellowship in
the love of God was threatened.

Then came the Black Manifesto. Adopted at the April 1969 conference on Black economic development of the Inter-Religious
Foundation for Community Organization, held at Detroit, the
manifesto asserted:

> For centuries we have been forced to live as colonized
> people inside the United States, victimized by the most vi-
> cious, racist system in the world. We have helped to build
> the most industrial country in the world. We are therefore
> demanding of the white Christian churches and Jewish
> synagogues which are part and parcel of the system of
> capitalism, that they begin to pay reparations to black
> people in this country. We are demanding $500,000,000
> from Christian white churches and the Jewish synagogues.
> This total comes to 15 dollars per nigger....[14]

On May 1st, James Foreman arrived at the Episcopal Church Center in New York to present the demands of the Black Manifesto. On May 13th he wrote to Presiding Bishop Hines demanding 60 million dollars immediately to fund the program of the Black Economic Development Conference, 60% each year of profits on assets, and an accounting of the total assets of the Episcopal Church in all dioceses.

Episcopal Church leaders were stunned. A siege atmosphere began to build and plans were made, in cooperation with civil officials, for dealing with the possibility of unfriendly occupation of churches and church offices. The concept of reparations was resented and all but universally rejected. Some denounced the manifesto altogether, while others pled for calm consideration of what the manifesto was really saying, justifying its tone on the basis of long-standing injustice and suffering. A Special Convention was called and met at Notre Dame from August 31 to September 5, 1969, where a positive response took shape, involving vigorous debate, and with awareness that Black clerical and lay delegates took the manifesto seriously. A special fund of $200,000 was voted for Black clergy to dispense to what was then known as the Black Economic Development Corporation. The convention did not think that by making this grant it was endorsing the concept of reparations. The grant reflected, rather, "the determination of the Episcopal Church—to the eradication of racial injustice in our land and in our Church. The focus was upon present and future attitudes and actions rather than upon the acknowledgement of a right to compensation for injuries in the past."[15]

After Notre Dame came the backlash. The withholding of funds from the national church grew until it was necessary to cut back severely both personnel and program at the Episcopal Church Center. Some Episcopalians left the church, joining the exodus already begun.[16] Some of those reacting against Notre Dame revealed strong racial prejudice. Others were reacting to what they saw as rampant liberalism evolving into dangerous radicalism, threatening the political/economic stability of the nation.

There was some truth in this latter accusation, evidenced by a movement toward more radical criticism of American society. Up to the mid-1960s Martin Luther King, Jr. had believed that American society was capable of reforming itself through legislation outlawing discrimination and guaranteeing voting rights. But he was discouraged by the ineffectiveness of legislation and began to recognize links between economic and social issues. King then called for a radical redistribution of economic and political power. His focus was on society as a whole and it was a short step for him to take from radical criticism of an economy that seemed to exacerbate the sufferings of the poor to leadership in the anti-war movement, protesting a war that seemed to exploit the poor Blacks.[17] Although accused by some of advocating a socialist, or even communist, alternative to capitalism, King argued that he was taking seriously the teachings of the Kingdom of God and urging that Christians regain control of their lives as a people of God and build, in the language we have been using, a fellowship in the love of God, dedicated to reconciliation.

What was being challenged was blind faith in a society whose systems tended to perpetuate racial discrimination, the oppression of the poor, and the ever-escalating arms race. The criticism could be applied, and was applied, equally to Soviet Russia and to other nations. While the praises of the socio-technical society were sung, and there was ample reason for rejoicing, the flaws could not be ignored. Langdon Gilkey, the theologian, has written:

A technological society makes us live and work publicly in ever larger corporate systems to whose demands we must conform if we are to participate. To them we subordinate our individuality, our conscience, our creativity, and our powers of self-expression and creative decision—those aspects of our humanity which make us human, whose loss strips us of our human being, and whose absence in the public life of society spells the doom of freedom and so of genuine participation in that society. It tends, unless resisted, to make our private leisure world equally empty of personal, individual, and creative content, a passive, senseless world devoid of spirit.[18]

Such an analysis gave rise to the conviction that if society is to preserve the values embodied in the Constitution and is to provide a setting in which a fellowship in the love of God can exist and grow, vigilance is required. Such vigilance is looked for in the church as the watchman, the prophetic critic of society. Jay W. Forrester, the developer of systems dynamics (a means of determining the bases on which we act as humans in society), believed that for society the responsibility for setting and maintaining long-range values rests with religion, specifically with the church. "The institution with the longest time horizon is in the best technical position to lead in exploring the nature of the social system; the church should establish that distant horizon. Long-term values are closely tied to what society is to be one hundred, or two hundred, or one thousand years hence. If not the church, who is to look ahead?" But, as Forrester went on to say, "the church is in the predicament of undergoing a shortening time horizon when it should be turning attention to a horizon beyond that of any other unit in the society."[19]

The critique, then, rightly turns to the church and its too great concentration on the immediate—a further dimension inherent in the criticism of those alarmed by the General Convention Special Program and its consequences. For some it seemed as though the Episcopal Church was simply responding to the most recent trends of society rather than providing leadership, or fixing its sights on the future hope and acting in accordance with that hope.

That the Episcopal Church was in fact providing leadership was demonstrated in the 1980s. In February of 1980 some 500 activist Episcopalians "brought to life the Episcopal Urban Caucus to address the needs of city people and parishes in the decades ahead. They met in Indianapolis at the call of the Urban Bishops Coalition and the Church and City Conference to study energy, the arms race, parish rehabilitation, and economic justice and to make recommendations for action."[20] In 1982 the Standing Commission on the Church in Metropolitan Areas of General Convention, begun in 1973 as a Joint Commission, working with the Episcopal Urban Caucus, inaugurated the Jubilee Ministry. This was designed to be "a celebrative ministry, based on our belief that by affirming the biblical priorities of God—in partnership with the poor, the powerless, the vulnerable—we discover our own humanity in Christ, our own freedom. It will be," the Commission went on to say, "a celebration of the Way of Jesus, a celebration that we live, not by the old order which is passing away, but by the New Creation, lighted by the vision of the City of God." The ministry was to be concerned for the cities, yet was determined to draw no distinctions "between rural, suburban, or urban." It was to focus upon consciousness raising, the designation and support of Jubilee Centers, training for needed special skills and much else.[21]

The program started slowly, but by 1985 there were forty Jubilee Centers. The Commission found them to be strongest in expressing compassion, "with few ministries designed to help the poor person in crisis to move from indignity to dignity, from exigency to stability. Even fewer Centers are finding ways to empower poor people to change the systemic faults, the injustices, which permit poverty to exist in an affluent society."[22] But the very recognition of such limitations and such deficiency in the program indicates concern for long range goals such as the church could provide. The 1982 report of the Commission was an important statement, with manifold implications for the future life and mission of the church. Theologically it emphasized the doctrine of the Incarnation, saying:

> We believe that in the Church's doctrine of the Incarnation we come face to face with our mission. Christ dwells among the least of our brothers and sisters; Christ dwells *in* the least of our brothers and sisters. Our response to their need is our action to God.... Failing to take seriously the doctrine of the Incarnation distorts our faith. Ignoring the implications for the earth since it has become God's dwelling place, we mistreat its resources and its fragile balance of life. Forgetting the image of God borne by each member of the human family, we denigrate and overlook them. Misunderstanding the importance which God places on the *human*, and on the human family as the People of God, we view salvation as a private affair. The sacraments, which celebrate God's presence in and through this world, lose their meaning.[23]

Women's Liberation

Episcopalians were further jolted by the women's movement beginning in the 1960s. Charles Willie, lay educator and church leader, pointed out that there was a connection between the civil rights movement and the women's movement, in that they were both freedom movements and both, finding their hopes unfulfilled, engaged in forceful action. Preaching at the ordination to the priesthood in 1974 in Philadelphia of twelve women of the Episcopal Church, Willie said: "As blacks refused to participate in their own oppression by going to the back of the bus in 1955 in Montgomery, women are refusing to cooperate in their own oppression by remaining on the periphery of full participation in the Church in 1974 in Philadelphia."[24]

The women's movement was inspired, in part, by the civil rights movement, sharing similar goals and strategies, but the

women separated from the civil rights movement when it became clear that many Black leaders treated them as inferiors.
When Carmichael said that "the only position for women in
SNCC is prone," women were enraged. Similar treatment was
experienced in the anti-war movement, one SDS speaker in 1965
observing that at the SDS convention that year "women made
peanut butter, waited on table, cleaned up, got laid. That was
their role."[25] By 1967 the women's movement began to thrive as
a separate entity. Working through the National Organization for
Women (NOW) and other groups, women challenged male
dominance in society, strove to make gains in personal freedom
and dignity, and worked to gain entrance into jobs and professions regarded as male preserves. By 1975, however, professional
women were still receiving only 73% of salaries paid to professional men and significant numbers were prevented from rising
above junior levels. Among the less skilled, the level of discrimination appeared to be unchanged. Furthermore, what social scientists called "the feminization of poverty" was becoming
a widely acknowledged fact. Underlying this poverty was a massive increase in female-headed households. In the 1970s there
was a 72% increase in the number of women heading households
with children. As William Chafe has observed: "The correlation
with poverty was direct and startling. A child born into a family
with no father in the house had one chance in three of being poor;
if a family was headed by a man alone, the chances of being poor
were one in ten; and if both parents were present, the chances
were one in nineteen."[26] The women's movement gained energy
from a worsening situation, a situation worsening even while efforts were being made to provide relief. As with Blacks in the
civil rights movement, women passed from hope to despair to
rage. The Episcopal Church was severely jolted as it felt the effects of that rage.

For years women had been struggling to achieve equality with
men in the councils of the church and had gradually made some
head way. In time women were admitted to serve on vestries, as

delegates to diocesan conventions, and finally as deputies to General Convention. At the time when the women's movement of the 70s was taking shape, with hope yielding to despair and rage, public attention was given to the place of women in the church's ministry. In 1966 the House of Bishops had been confronted by the need to address the question as to "whether or not women should be considered eligible for ordination to any and all Orders" of the church's ministry. The House of Bishops then requested the Lambeth Conference of the bishops of the Anglican Communion to consider the question in 1968. At Lambeth the bishops approved the ordination of women to the diaconate, but turned the question of ordination to the priesthood and consecration to the episcopate back to the provinces. In 1970 the Joint Commission on Ordained and Licensed Ministries recommended to the General Convention meeting in Houston that all orders of ministry be opened immediately to women. The recommendation was rejected in the House of Deputies by a narrow margin but received the support of the Triennial Meeting of Episcopal Church Women by a vote of 222 to 45.[27]

From 1970 on the issue was arduously joined. In the midst of the struggle the existence of the church as a fellowship in the love of God, dedicated to reconciliation was being tested, if not brought into question. The House of Bishops in October 1970, after vigorous discussion and the revelation of severe divisions in their ranks on the issue, referred this statement to the House of Deputies: "It is the mind of this House that it endorses the principle of the Ordination of Women to the Priesthood and the Ordination and Consecration of Women to the Episcopate."[28]

The Presiding Bishop appointed a committee, chaired by Stephen Bayne, to consider the statement and to report to the House in October 1972, in preparation for the General Convention of 1973. The committee, composed of two bishops known to favor the ordination of women, two opposed, and three uncommitted, produced a learned report but made no specific recommendations. Although it was "not prepared to say with one mind...that the Church should open all its orders of ministry to women," nevertheless, the report did say:

> The issue of liberation must be seen and taken in utter seriousness and in very great depth, even as the men in Jerusalem took the issue of the Gentiles. The cause of the liberation of men and women in the sense that we see it and describe it is not going to be served by token readjustment of quotas and the like. Nor will the Church and we who rejoice in the Church be cleansed by the confrontation if we do not deeply share its pain and its hope, and open every possible door to the full partnership of men and women in the Church's life. If the Church has, as the Committee unitedly believes, a peculiar mission to men and women caught in the perplexities of our society and struggling to learn how to become what they really are, the Church must seize every way it finds to re-establish lost credibility and to take the initiative and to regain its capacity to serve its mission in contemporary humanity.[29]

In a note appended to the report some members of the committee expressed their conviction that female imagery as well as male imagery was applicable to the priesthood and that Christ's priesthood was too comprehensive to be restricted to the symbolism of one sex. They thus opened the way for theological reflection and concluded that they might be on the threshold of "a new dimension and awareness of the unsearchable riches of Christ." "Far from confusing sexual roles or affirming unisex values," they asked, "might not the ordination of women assume the enrichment of our understanding of humanity in Christ by guaranteeing the presence of both its components visibly present in the offering of the Oblation which is Christ's and ours?"[30]

Opposition to the ordination of women on biblical and theological grounds was also to be found in the report. The New Testament, it was stated, gives no evidence of women as bishop-presbyters. Theologically, the Christian priest, it was argued, "is a sacrament of the recreative act of God towards mankind." This is symbolized on the human level "in masculinity as biologically expressed in the male. A woman priest, therefore, must lack the full symbolic expression of the meaning of Christian priesthood, and to that extent must be defective." There was also concern expressed at the thought that the Episcopal Church might act to ordain women contrary to the practice of other churches. "This momentous step must not be taken by a small branch of a particular Catholic Church on its own initiative, without reference to the remainder of catholic Christendom, and I am sure, against the convictions and sentiments of a majority of its own members."[31]

The issue and the issues were debated by the House of Bishops and the statement made at Houston endorsing the ordination of women was approved by a vote of 75 to 61 with 5 absentions. There was maneuvering behind the scenes, pro and con, aimed at forcing a decision at Louisville in 1973. However, it was not until 1976, after the dramatic action of the twelve women at Philadelphia, that the deed was done, loudly acclaimed by many, denounced by others, more people leaving the Episcopal Church, joining others to be found in Anglican splinter groups.

The formal, legal end to discrimination against women in the Episcopal Church had many ramifications, including changes in language and imagery, changes in the way history is perceived and theology done. In addressing the common statement that "God is male toward humanity: humanity is female toward God," Samuel Wylie, bishop of Northern Michigan, and author of a pro-ordination paper in the 1972 report, wrote (drawing on André Dumas' *Concerning the Ordination of Women*, WCC, 1964):

The cardinal truth is that the religion of Yahweh came into existence in the midst of a galaxy of myths [concerning gods as supermen and superwomen who in coupling create the heavens and the earth] and from the very begin-

ning rejected them. Yahweh was alone. To pluck phrases
from Prof. Dumas again, "Yahweh is the Creator; but He is
never the procreator, as Baal was, in the form of a bull (Exodus 32, 1 Kings 12:28–30). The Person of God is completely severed from the web of myths and rites which
worshipped sexuality. God is unique, which means that He
is not in the likeness of man, nor of woman, nor of them
together." As in the Priestly Creation story (Genesis 1) man
and woman together are in the image of God; He holds both
maleness and femaleness in Himself, yet He is not limited
to them or by them.

This is a corrective reflection, not an attempt to say that
male or female imagery is automatically untrue in human
experience. There is a giving-ness about God which we call
love or revelation or providence, and it is in the sense of the
divine initiative in that which we, in our habitual cultural
milieu, commonly associate with the responsible initiative
of male figures—husband, father. Indeed we come honestly by both these images. There is, equally, a notion of
humanity's receiving God's gifts which, again quite under-
standably, we commonly associate with female figures—
wife, daughter.

The point here is not to attempt to rule out the reality of
such imagery, but rather to see it in both its power and its
limitations.[32]

As Black theology accompanied Black power, so feminist
theology accompanied the women's movement. Such theology
involved men like Dumas and Wylie, but it was chiefly the work
of women theologians and varied greatly from woman to
woman, from the radical critique of Mary Daly to the more
restrained reasoning of Rosemary Ruether. All were united in
identifying feminist theology as theology of revolution, to which
Letty Russell has pointed. Feminist theology called upon all of

the people of God to accept their common status, their equality as the children of God, God who is beyond identification with the particularities of human sexuality, God whose influence works in and through the entire creation, reconciling the divided, overcoming fragmentation, restoring that wholism which is a prime characteristic of the holy.[33]

Feminist theology is a type of liberation theology, although it might differ from specific liberation theologies. As a liberation theology it insists that the people of God must be vigilant against forces in society that would subsume and transform Christianity, making the church into a tool for the power brokers. Rosemary Ruether spoke of the need to cleanse the church, that it might be that which it was made to be. Cleansed, it is powerful to effect change.

> The exorcism of the demonic spirit of sexism in the church touches off a revolution which must transform all the relations of alienation and domination—between self and body, between leaders and community, between person and person, between social groups, between church and world, between humanity and nature, finally our model of God in relation to creation—all of which have been modelled on our sexist schizophrenia.[34]

Women's liberation is thus not a side-issue. The "exorcism of the demonic spirit of sexism in the church" is essential if the church is to become a fellowship in the love of God, whose mission is an ever growing sphere of an ever deepening reconciliation.

In the 1980s the problem of the deployment of women priests is acknowledged as critical. Pressure grows to elect, ordain and consecrate women as bishops, in fulfillment of the action taken by General Convention in 1976. In 1985 the House of Bishops resolved that "the majority of the members of this House do not intend to withhold consent to the election of a Bishop of this Church on grounds of gender." They called upon the Presiding

Bishop to "communicate this intention to the Primates of the Anglican Communion" and to seek their advice.[35] The House of Deputies asked that the Presiding Bishop appoint a special committee to "study and make recommendations concerning the ecumenical- ecclesiological considerations involved in the election and ordination of women Presbyters to the Episcopate."[36]

It was obvious that there was still opposition to the ordination of women. A meeting of so-called "traditionalist" Anglican bishops was held at Fairfield, Connecticut in March, 1986, led by Graham Leonard, Bishop of London. A report said that they "were rallying to coordinate their strategy for world-wide opposition to the ordination of women. They also talked of relations with Rome and the Orthodox Churches; of the danger of Anglican schism; and of the possible healing of American schisms."[37] Also in March 1986 the Primates of the Anglican Communion met in Toronto, Canada, and there suggested that the Episcopal Church in the U.S.A. exercise "some restraint" over the matter of electing a woman to the episcopate—"until discussions by the episcopate at the 1988 Lambeth Conference."[38]

Meanwhile, more and more women were being ordained to the presbyterate and assuming positions of responsibility. Women's ordination was a fact. The church was learning to live with that fact and to fulfill the promises made by General Convention in 1976 and following.

The Church and the Vietnam War

The years of crisis for the Episcopal Church were greatly affected by the Cold War and by such "hot" wars as those in Korea in the 50s and in Southeast Asia in the 60s and 70s. American involvement in Vietnam was especially critical, arousing as it did massive reactions from peaceful demonstrations to civil disobedience and riots. Beginning with the economic aid and military advice supplied to anti-communists during the presidencies of Truman and Eisenhower, American involvement escalated with the French defeat at Dien Bien Phu in 1954. An American commitment to intervene, contain communism in Asia, and supply economic and military assistance to any country threatened by "overt armed aggression from any nation controlled by international communism." With the enactment in Congress of the Gulf of Tonkin resolution in 1964, authorizing President Johnson "to take *all* necessary measures to repel *any* armed attack against the forces of the United States," full-scale military engagement commenced with hundreds of thousands of combat and support military personnel struggling against great odds to save an unstable anti-communist government.[39]

Before a peace settlement was signed in January 1973, thousands of Americans were dead, millions of Southeast Asians had been killed, the land had been bombed and burned, unspeakable crimes against humanity had been committed, and countless numbers of Americans, engaged in what was publicly decreed to be a fruitless effort, were brutalized, driven to drugs and insanity by the sheer brutality of their existence in "the big muddy." The horror of the search and destroy mission at the village of My Lai was to haunt Americans for a generation and more.

The reaction in the Episcopal Church, as in other churches, was severely divided between those convinced of the necessity of the war in Southeast Asia and those opposed to it and to American involvement in any form. A.T. Mollegen, the theologian, spoke for many when he endorsed the domino theory as expounded by John Foster Dulles and others, arguing that if Vietnam fell to the communists all of Asia would fall in time. Episcopalian members of Clergy and Laymen Concerned about Vietnam and those belonging to the Episcopal Peace Fellowship objected to such reasoning, pointing to the mass destruction of civilian populations— ignored by theorists. "Our military presence in Vietnam, far from stemming the tide of communism, serves rather to unite more firmly those communist societies which might otherwise develop separate destinies," stated Clergy and Laymen Concerned about Vietnam in February 1967.[40] Mass demonstrations were held, especially in Washington; young men resisted the draft, some of them publicly destroying their draft cards; seminaries began to receive men seeking refuge. Violence erupted sporadically, culminating in open warfare between police and demonstrators in 1968 at the Democratic National Convention in Chicago, and in the devastating attack of Ohio National Guardsmen on students gathered at Kent State University in 1970 to protest the invasion of Cambodia by the United States.

More specifically, how did the Episcopal Church react? In different ways, for the members of the fellowship disagreed. Officially the General Convention reaffirmed the Lambeth Conference 1930 statement "that war as a method of settling international disputes is incompatible with the teaching and example of our Lord Jesus Christ."[41] This position was the general rule. Conscientious objection to service in war and the limits of civil obedience were recognized by the House of Bishops and General Convention in the 1960s, the House of Bishops being readier to endorse such positions than the House of Deputies. At General Convention in 1967 a specific statement on Vietnam was made, illuminating the church's self-understanding. It said, in part:

> We know that we are members, one of another, and that in the face of our common extremity and the apocalyptic danger of our time, each man is responsible for all men, that what each man is or does makes a difference to the fate of all men, that all mankind will survive together or go under together.[42]

The statement recognized that the church is involved in the world and that in "its being and mission" it has a duty "to speak out of conscience in matters of faith and morals." This, it was believed, was certainly true where Vietnam was concerned. The 1967 statement then said:

> It is the essence of the Christian faith that all men and all nations come under the judgment of God and are required to live in peace and justice and with due regard for the rights and dignity of every human being.
>
> War is madness. It is the scourge, the disease of all mankind. War is obsolete and if life is to continue on earth, all nations and all men must forthwith and without delay seek to accomplish its complete elimination as an instrument of national policy.
>
> We hear the cry of all people, of mothers and fathers, wives and widows, the old generation and the new, crying for peace on earth. Particularly are we moved by the suffering of the people of Vietnam. War always brings suffering but in Vietnam the suffering is intensified because Vietnamese fights Vietnamese, there are few fixed battle lines, and friend and foe, combatant and civilian are often indistinguishable. We acknowledge our share in the affliction and suffering.[43]

At the end of the Seattle Convention twenty-four bishops called for an end to "the undeclared war in Vietnam as soon as possible."

One of those who heeded the General Convention's message was Cotesworth Pinkney Lewis, rector of Bruton Parish Church in Williamsburg, Virginia. On November 12, 1967, the President of the United States, Lyndon Johnson, attended church in Williamsburg. Lewis preached a sermon on Isaiah 9:2, and in the midst of his sermon spoke of Vietnam. "The political complexities of our involvement in an undeclared war in Vietnam are so baffling that I feel presumptuous even in asking questions," he said. But with the realization that there was a widespread conviction that there was something wrong in Vietnam, he proceeded to ask questions:

Relatively few of us plan even the mildest form of disloyal action against constituted authority. "United we stand, divided we fall." We know the necessity of supporting our leader. But we cannot close our Christian consciences to consideration of the rightness of actions as they are reported to us,—perhaps erroneously, perhaps for good cause (of which we have not been apprised). We are appalled that apparently this is the only war in our history which has had three times as many civilian as military casualties. It is particularly regrettable that to so many nations the struggle's purpose appears as neo-colonialism. We are mystified by news accounts suggesting that our brave fighting units are inhibited by directives and inadequate equipment for using their capacities to terminate the conflict successfully.

While pleading our loyalty—we ask humbly, WHY?

This sermon, delivered by a man who could in no way be construed to be a radical, proved to be a landmark in the course of events. The reactions to it were swift and decisive. Lewis was both praised and damned. He became the center of national attention. The Governor of Virginia apologized to the President for the rector's remarks. The Bishop of Southern Virginia defended Lewis but expressed the opinion that the rector spoke as an individual and not for the Episcopal Church or the diocese. Lewis was denounced in Congress and in his own congregation. The Vestry of Bruton Parish apologized to the President for "the discourtesy shown him." The rector commented that the vestry's action "has given me great confidence." He explained: "These gentlemen acted as their consciences directed them to, just as I acted as my conscience directed me." Lewis understood something of the church as a fellowship in which there can be disagree-

ment because there is love. It is of interest to note that when the
New York Times reported the President's decision not to seek re-
election, it said Johnson "guessed the turning point in his thinking about the next four years came last November..."[44]

The issue for the church in all of the struggles of the time was
that of being what it was created to be, a fellowship in the love
of God whose mission and ministry is reconciliation. The issue
extended to consideration of the church in the midst of conflict
among nations and with differing views as to the conflicts within
a particular church. At the World Council of Churches' Oxford
Conference in 1937, this statement was made, one that was
remembered more than once during the Vietnam war:

> The universal Church, surveying the nations of the
> world...must pronounce a condemnation of war un-
> qualified and unrestricted...If war breaks out, then pre-
> eminently the Church must manifestly be the Church, still
> united as the one Body of Christ, though the nations
> wherein it is planted fight each other, consciously offering
> the same prayers that God's name may be hallowed, his
> Kingdom come, and His will be done in both, or all, the
> warring nations. This fellowship of prayer must at all costs
> remain unbroken. The Church must also hold together in
> one spiritual fellowship those of its members, who take dif-
> ferent views concerning their duty as Christian citizens in
> time of war.[45]

In the 1980s the church's mission of reconciliation involved
General Convention support for the Camp David Accords and
concern for "the right of Palestinian people to exercise responsibility for their political future, with the proviso that the Pales-
tinians recognize the legitimacy of the State of Israel."[46]

Opposition to United States policy in Central America and
support for the Contadora initiative was expressed.[47] In 1982
first use of nuclear weapons was strongly opposed, as was Presi-

dent Reagan's Strategic Defense Initiative (SDI) in 1985; the General Convention requested Congress "to withhold funds for study of the feasibility of this proposed 'umbrella' that some contend could be built to remove the threat of nuclear war."[48]

Such resolutions on the part of General Convention did not represent all points of view in the church, but were in accord with the general policies of the Episcopal Church, the Anglican Communion, and the World Council of Churches. Most important in terms of ideology and education was the 1982 report of the Joint Commission on Peace, called *To Make Peace*, a careful, balanced, and yet forthright document, not advocating pacifism but clearly stating: "Responsible patriotism demands our involvement in the work of peace. Even more profoundly our Christian faith calls us to the same work." The task was seen as one of incarnating the gospel: loving our enemies. Said the report:

> To love our nation's enemies is today as difficult as it is urgent. Nevertheless, to avoid dehumanizing stereotypes, to see to it that what peacetime good we do is done impartially, to champion justice self-critically on our side of any growing hostilities, and even in hostilities to continue doing good to those who may hate us, these are specific and concrete actions clearly expected of us according to the scripture. They do not measure up to the sacrificial love Christians may hope to show to enemies in isolated, purely person-to-person relations. Nor do they rule out the sometimes necessary use of organized force in the service of justice and peace. But they do describe an attitude, a perspective, an intentionality which should inform our actions toward "enemies" even in the midst of conflict, when the possibilities for peace and reconciliation seem most remote.[49]

The Charismatic Movement

Alongside the engagement of the Episcopal Church in societal crises during the 1960s there developed the charismatic movement, no longer restricted to pentecostal sects but growing within mainline churches in America. This phenomenon was variously regarded as a reaction against social activism, a response to the superficiality of Christianity within secular culture, an attempt to fill a long standing need in the churches that had neglected the doctrine of the Holy Spirit, or a form of social introversion or social hysteria.

The charismatic movement was defined by Michael Hamilton, a canon of Washington Cathedral, as a movement of those who "experienced a 'baptism of the Holy Spirit' that involves certain spiritual gifts." Chief among the gifts was tongue-speaking or glossalalia, but there were also gifts of prophecy and healing. There was "a desire for an active style of participatory worship in which these gifts are practiced. Through enthusiastic evangelism, the movement...found support not only in local congregations, but also on university campuses, in newly founded residential communities, and in various types of societies."[50] The laity were much involved, but there were also numerous clergy in the movement.

Kilian McDonnell has described the charismatic phenomenon as a movement of prophetic renewal. "To a large degree its prophetic protest and its renewal goals are directed to the churches," where people tend to live below the expected spiritual potential, devoid of any real sense of Christ's presence in worship and daily life, lacking joy and peace and hope. The charismatic movement sought to provide what was lacking. In this sense it was a prophetic renewal movement.[51]

The beginnings of the movement in the Episcopal Church are associated with Richard Winkler, rector of Trinity Church, Wheaton, Illinois, who, influenced by a Methodist layman named Dunscombe, received baptism in the Holy Spirit on April 26, 1956, and made his church into a center of charismatic renewal. Dennis Bennett, rector of St. Mark's Church, Van Nuys, California, who received baptism in the Holy Spirit in November 1959, gained national attention when, in April 1960, some seventy of his parishioners received the pentecostal experience and he announced to his congregation what had happened. The parish was divided, one of his curates stormed out of the church, the church treasurer suggested that the rector resign, which he did, and the bishop prohibited pentecostal activity in the diocese. Bennett had learned of baptism in the Spirit from a neighboring priest. It was becoming evident that baptism in the Spirit and tongues-speaking were spreading in the church.

James W. Jones, an Episcopal priest/theologian at Rutgers University, and a sympathetic interpreter of the movement, argued in 1974 that the charismatic movement arose and grew spontaneously. "The neo-Pentecostals appeared," he said, "not through proselytizing efforts on the part of classical pentecostals...but when groups of Protestants met together to deepen *their* spiritual lives."[52]The intensity of the need, among people who felt the deprivations of secularity and religious aridity, opened them to the working of the Spirit in ways largely unexpected, totally surprising. The way toward neo-Pentecostalism in the Episcopal Church was prepared through the healing ministries of people such as Agnes Sanford and the evangelical piety of people such as Samuel Shoemaker, but it could still be argued, as it was by Jones, that it was fundamentally spontaneous.

Official reactions were at first largely negative. In relation to the case of Dennis Bennett, a commission appointed by Bishop Francis Bloy of Los Angeles, reported in April 1960, expressing doubt as to the normality, in psychological terms, of the phenomenon of tongues-speaking as related in Acts 2.[53] The commission appointed by Bishop Francis Burrill of Chicago, as a result of the Winkler affair, concluded in December 1960 that there was danger that tongues-speaking might be exaggerated, "especially when it is viewed in isolation and separation from the wholeness of God's inspiration." The commission further saw a threat of sectarianism in the movement and argued that Christians ought to submit their experience to the church and to reason which "is supremely the voice of the Holy Ghost," operative in the counsels of the church.[54]

The report of a commission appointed by Bishop Pike of California in 1963 spoke of tongues-speaking and its dangers, of the tendency among some charismatics toward biblical fundamentalism, and of an unhealthy subjectivism among those of the movement. But it regarded the emphasis on Scripture as a rebuke for "the great number of Episcopal congregations where serious Bible study is totally ignored by both clergy and laity," and viewed the tendency toward subjectivism as a corrective in the light of the ways in which Episcopalians "over-formalize and over-objectify the working of God." It furthermore acknowledged biblical precedents for glossalalia, but stated that "there is no scriptural warrant for making it normative for all Christians then or now."[55]

Bishop Pike, in a Pastoral Letter issued at the same time, "doubted whether religious categories and practices borrowed from classical Protestantism could be harmonized with the sacramental and priestly tradition of the Episcopal Church." In particular he objected to the "heavily subjective emphasis upon a personal relationship with Jesus," the indiscriminate laying on of hands, induced tongues, and the practice of speaking in tongues at public services.[56] Pike's concerns were echoed by James C. Logan who viewed American charismatics as individualistic and non-social, quite different from those in Brazil and Chile. "A renewal of individuals without the redemption of the society in which they must live," he wrote, "is hardly sufficient for the renewal of the church which is Christ's body broken and given for the life of the world."[57]

Of major consequence was the House of Bishops Pastoral Letter in 1971, which strove to maintain a positive view of the charismatic renewal and of its influence through Cursillo, Faith Alive, and other renewal agencies as they developed. The Pastoral stated that there was abundant evidence "of the movement of the Holy Spirit...in the lives of individuals and in the life of the church," and "a growing awareness of the pentecostal power of the Holy Spirit to transform men and women." The bishops affirmed that God "is working in the devotional lives of his people, and in their experience of his charismatic gifts of prayer, praise, and healing, and in their joy in the sacramental life." They went on to say, "We praise Him for showing us again that faith without works is dead, and that there can be no divorce between religious faith and active concern for justice and brotherhood." And so, they concluded, "We rejoice that He has called us to share in Christ's ministry of reconciliation."[58]

Through the 1970s and 1980s the renewal movement spread through the Episcopal Church. Cursillo was in some ways most prominent. Founded at Mallorca in Spain around 1949, the *Cursillo en Christianidad* ("a short course in Christianity") was designed to arouse somnolent Roman Catholics and to reinvigorate their parishes. Concentrated on a structured weekend (about which silence is maintained in order to preserve the surprise or shock value of the happenings)[59] more and more people underwent initiation, were maintained in a state of renewal by participation in *ultreyas*, regrouped initiates, and were trained for leadership. The movement spread world-wide and is represented in the Episcopal Church by a National Cursillo Committee. As has been said, "A cursillo weekend offers an awareness of the reality of God's love and the experience of Christian community as lived to its fullness."[60]

Faith Alive, founded in 1970, has affected hundreds of parishes in the Episcopal Church. Its aim, too, is parish renewal, with laypeople from miles around visiting a particular parish for a weekend, there to witness to the vitality of Christian experience in their lives.[61] Such movements are not without problems. The understanding of them can vary widely, especially in the Cursillo Movement which is so wide-spread. They are challenged to maintain the initial impact of the weekend, and are only partially successful in doing so. As in any movement, there is the danger of becoming exclusive as well as manipulative.[62]

But renewal was one major means of reforming the church as a fellowship in the love of God, whose mission is an ever growing sphere of a constantly deepening reconciliation.

In general it can be said that there was amongst many people in the 1960s, 70s and 80s a fresh appreciation of the Third Person of the Trinity. Such appreciation was not limited to charismatics. It increasingly influenced the thought of church leaders in general. The Holy Spirit in the thought of John Taylor (at one time executive of the Church Missionary Society and later the Bishop of Winchester in England) is identified as the "Go-between God" who creates fellowship with God and amongst the people of God. "What *causes* the fellowship," wrote Taylor in 1973, "is the gift of awareness which opens our eyes to one another, makes us see as we never saw before, the secret of all evolution, the spark that sets off most revolution, the dangerous life-giver, the Holy Spirit."[63]

It was apparent that in the midst of the strife of a chaotic time there was emerging a new sensitivity and openness to the Holy Spirit, involving a recognition that the Spirit works through diverse people creating fellowship in the love of God and impelling people into the world, to be agents of reconciliation. In and through the civil rights movement, the women's movement, the anti-war movement, the radical theologies of the 1960s and the liberation theologies of the 1970s, the walls of separation in church and society were being broken down, hearts were being broken open, God beyond the god of human invention was being made known that the Holy Spirit might work to reform the church, renewing it as a fellowship in the love of God.

The Kingdom of God is realized proleptically as rich and poor, male and female, black and brown and white and red, Jew and Gentile, sit down at God's table to feed one another. As we approach this realization of the messianic banquet we experience the growing, deepening reconciliation of those fragmented within and divided from one another. This is the reconciliation of the individual with God through repentance, forgiveness and thanksgiving; reconciliation of person with person through mutual love and forgiveness. It is a deepening reconciliation in the sense that the veiled spirits of people are drawn forth out of darkness and brought into fellowship, the fellowship of the saints of God everlasting.

Chapter 3

The Episcopal Church and Global Issues

The "Shrinking" Earth

One of the most dramatic and important revelations of the years beginning in 1950 was the fact that in many ways the planet earth was "shrinking." By the time Neil Armstrong set foot on the moon, people had seen pictures taken of the earth from outer space, the earth appearing to be no more than a small, agate ball suspended in vast nothingness, sustained by tenuous, unseen forces, with life dependent upon a relatively thin, fragile envelope of atmosphere. It is still difficult to comprehend the vastness of space in which our planet is no more than a mere speck. William Barrett has said: "Our ingenious species has now traveled to the moon. But what is the distance to the moon, but the tiniest bubble in the ocean of our galaxy, which in turn is but a bubble in the ocean of space that engulfs it?"[1]

Those sensitive to such perceptions, could no longer perceive earth as the dominant center of the universe. Its importance seemed to dwindle as our knowledge increased. Furthermore, as years went by more and more people came to appreciate the fact that although divided into many nations, they lived in close proximity to one another, their lives interdependent in a multitude of ways. There was the development of world-wide com-

munications networks, making use of satellites in space. There
was the increasing speed, efficiency, and affordability of air
travel. There was the growing inter-connectedness of national
economies not only through the growth in number and prestige
of multi-national corporations but also through sophisticated
banking and international trade relations. Something that happened in one place could have ramifications in distant parts of
the earth. A failed harvest in the U.S.S.R. resulted in the export
of vast amounts of grain out of the United States, sharply higher
meat prices for increasingly disgruntled Americans, and a worsening of starvation in the Indian subcontinent for lack of grain
from the United States: the available supplies had gone to the
Soviet Union.[2] The Arab oil embargo of the 1970s affected people
around the world, not abstractly, but practically; not only in
terms of fuel oil, but also in oil-related industries and national
economies as well.[3] Scientists pointed out how damage to the
environment in one place could have disastrous effects elsewhere. Acid rain from the United States poisoned Canadian
waters and forests, endangering fish resources and threatening
timber lands on which important segments of the Canadian
economy depended. In the 1970s scientists began to suspect that
the ozone layer, without which no life on earth could survive,
was being damaged and cautioned against the use of fluorocar-
bons in such things as aerosol sprays. In December 1984, a toxic
cloud drifted from the Union Carbide plant in Bhopal, India, kill-
ing 2,000 people, warning of similar fatal accidents ready to occur
in other parts of the world. And in April 1986 an accident at the
Chernobyl nuclear power plant in Russia spread harmful radia-
tion across Europe, carried on upper-level winds over the
Arabian Peninsula, Siberia, and North America.

In addition, there was a growing awareness of the interdependence of the people on earth in terms of the cold war and the
arms race. When Sputnik was launched by a Soviet intercon-
tinental missile in 1957, Nikita Krushchev boasted that such a
missile could accurately be directed to any part of the planet.

Shortly the United States, and then others, were to boast of a similar capability. The entire planet was then vulnerable and the United Nations took on increased significance as a forum in which potential dangers to the survival of earth could be discussed. As the arms race proceeded there were those who argued that a massive war was now out of the question, the very magnitude of the threat guaranteeing peace. But the threat remained. The possibility of nuclear holocaust continued to loom over us, and it was little solace to be told by authorities that five to fifteen percent of earth's population could survive a full-scale nuclear war.

The earth, in terms of such realities, was indeed shrinking. At the same time, those concerned focused much of their attention on the need to perceive the reality of a shrinking world and adjust not only attitudes but structures to the new reality. At the World Conference on Church and Society held at Geneva, Switzerland, in 1966, Dr. Max Kohnstamm asked:

> How can there be an ordered, peaceful world as long as the structures are outdated? As long as each separate human community lives according to its own laws and no others? The world is like a jungle with each nation a "cold beast" prowling around devouring whom it can. We know that justice and order within a nation depends upon the establishment of just laws and institutions and coercive power; how then can man ever develop a just and ordered world community without the same basic essentials, applied universally? Yet such structures hardly exist at all today and the Christian is called to maintain the ones that do (the United Nations for one) and to develop new ones—to find the "cracks" in the hard pan of present world systems and plant there the seeds of new structures[4]

Church leaders all over the world recognized the challenge before them and summoned their people to help them meet the challenge of a shrinking world.

The Anglican Communion and the World Mission

The Episcopal Church in this era came to see itself more and more as interdependent in its relationship to other churches of the Anglican Communion and other denominations, Protestant, Orthodox, and Roman Catholic. In 1959 Stephen Bayne, then Bishop of Olympia in the state of Washington, accepted an appointment as the first executive officer of the Anglican Communion. At the 1958 Lambeth Conference such an appointment had been called for in part because the bishops realized that new conditions, requiring new relationships, were developing in the world, affecting the then eighteen autonomous churches of the Anglican Communion, churches related to the See of Canterbury and enjoying the benefits of intercommunion. Bayne began traveling, as much as 150,000 miles a year, chiefly by air, passing from continent to continent in hours, reaching to every part of the earth. He began to sense how small earth was and to realize that although one did not cease to be an American or a Pakistani, yet as a human being he belonged to a global community and as a Christian was a participant in the Kingdom of God, a kingdom that knows no national divisions or exclusive spheres of influence.

To be a member of the body that is the People of God, Bayne believed, is to be related in the most intimate bonds of faith to all people who profess Christ to be Lord and Master whether they be Oriental or Caucasian, capitalist or communist, above the equator or below, rich or poor. A Christian by virtue of being a Christian could never be narrowly American or Pakistani. His reasoning led him to the conclusion that true patriotism inspires people to a greater vision and greater loyalty, beyond the native land, the particular race, the specific gender.[5] And for one who traveled as much as he did, there remained the fact that in all parts of the earth there were followers of Christ, worshipping God in spirit and in truth, in a dazzling variety of tongues and dialects, Anglicans using one form or another of the *Book of Com-*

mon Prayer and the Holy Bible, translated into their own tongues but providing a vivid sense of belonging to one another.

The story of the Tower of Babel told of the fragmentation of humankind, people speaking different tongues and not understanding one another. The Bible also told of Pentecost, when, although people spoke different languages, they understood one another, their divisions were healed, and they were reconciled in the fellowship of God's people. Christianity, many believed, existed to promote reconciliation in the world. The time was ripe for the church to proceed on its mission of reconciliation, Christ's mission, the mission of Christ's own body, of which he is the head. As the earth seemed to shrink, that mission became ever clearer, for people were becoming more interdependent, more in need of reconciliation, if they were to survive. The danger was that through being brought into intimate, sometimes direct contact, people in their efforts to survive would destroy one another in competition for the earth's limited resources. Bayne and others chose to believe that a new sense of unity was finding expression on earth, a spirit that could overcome the dangers, and that the Anglican Communion would ignore the new reality and the new opportunities for mission at its own peril.

The inherited wisdom in the Anglican Communion, as in other communions, taught that there were those who sent money and personnel, and those who received them. The sending churches were older, the receiving churches were younger; the older churches were missionary, the younger churches were missions. This familiar situation was now being challenged. The nations of the Third World were working toward the development of economic and social systems in imitation of the First. At the same time there was movement toward indigenization (or "contextualization"— the word now preferred), reinforced by the overthrow of colonialism in Africa and elsewhere, accompanied by the expulsion of foreigners, including foreign missionaries. In Africa indigenization occurred at a time of spectacular growth. In the 1980s one began to hear of "Afro-Anglicanism" or "black

Anglicanism" and rapid expansion in the younger dioceses of Central Africa, Kenya, Sudan, Tanzania, and Uganda. With the numbers of Anglicans in England, Australia, the United States, and elsewhere falling, the Anglican Communion was changing. As John Pobee said, "Today, *ecclesia anglicana* is very international with only slightly more than one half of the total number of Episcopalians being White. The majority of the dioceses are not Anglo-Saxon. The majority of Anglicans are either non-native-speakers of English or non-speakers of English."[6] The trend toward this important development was already established in the 1960s.

In addition there was a waning of missionary zeal in the prosperous West, among traditional, so-called mainline denominations (unlike Pentecostals, Mormons, and the like, whose zeal was increasing). The time was ripe, as Bayne saw it, for a radically new perspective and thus he began to speak of mutual responsibility and interdependence. At a meeting of missionary executives in the summer of 1963, he spoke of responsibility, the need for careful planning, and for setting priorities based on such planning. "No one is independent," he said. "We must find ways in which this mutual planning can be developed. Each church has something to teach the others...No church ought to send anyone without asking in depth what it wants in return. Then the element of mutuality comes into existence."[7]

At this meeting the document "Mutual Responsibility and Interdependence in the Body of Christ" (MRI) began to take shape. When the document was presented at the Toronto Anglican Congress on August 17, 1963, it was with the realization that a revolution in thought and action was being proposed to all Anglican churches, including the Episcopal Church. The keynotes of the era, the document declared, are equality, interdependence, and mutual responsibility. In the light of this, and of the Gospel, the document redefined mission, the character of the Anglican Communion, and the new condition of equality prevailing among the formerly unequal churches of the communion:

The Church's mission is response to the living God who in his love creates, reveals, judges, redeems, fulfils. It is he who moves through our history to teach and to save, who calls us to receive his love, to learn, to obey and follow.

Our unity in Christ, expressed in our full communion, is the most profound bond among us, in all our political and racial and cultural diversity.

The time has fully come when this unity and interdependence must find a completely new level of expression and corporate obedience.[8]

The churches, including the Episcopal Church, were called upon in the succeeding weeks and months to study their needs and their resources and through mutual consultation and planning, with the setting of priorities, determine how best they might assist one another. Furthermore, it was expected that each church would engage in self-study, to "test and evaluate every activity in its life by the test of mission and of service to others, in our following after Christ." In the terms we have been using from John Knox, the churches were expected to test and evaluate every activity by the standard of the church as a fellowship in the love of God whose mission is to be the constantly growing sphere of a constantly deepening reconciliation. Mutuality concerns fellowship and interdependence concerns reconciliation; both mutuality and interdependence are expressive of all that is implied by responsible communion in the body of Christ.

From the outset, however, the "Mutuality and Interdependence" program was misinterpreted. Some regarded it as simply another money-raising scheme; Bayne protested that it was not.[9] Some opposed it as detracting from the church's involvement in the ecumenical movement; Bayne argued that the Anglican Communion itself was an adventure in ecumenism, properly understood.[10] The older churches were not inclined to give up their privileged positions as older and stronger churches sending money to younger and weaker churches that could not possibly have anything that their elders would need. Furthermore, the events of the time, the urban riots, the anti-war ferment, the struggles for liberation, over-shadowed what some persisted in calling the "missionary program." Bayne protested that the program was wholistic, involving every aspect of the church's life, and that it was applicable to urban America as well as to the deserts and jungles of Africa.[11] It would not be long, he believed, before the Third World was as industrialized as the First, such was the rapidity of change in the under-developed parts of the world.

The main issue, however, concerned the church's self-understanding. To his own sadness, Bayne had to recognize that the first responses to MRI made clear not only that First World churches were unwilling or unable to change, but that the Third World churches were also adhering to the older attitudes and structures. Bishops in Africa sat down and drew up a list of needs involving millions of dollars, without sufficient consideration of what *they* might give to meet the needs of the wealthy. The mission of the church was still viewed in terms of missionary work by selected, trained missionaries sent to foreign lands. Yet Bayne understood mission to be the chief work of Christians everywhere, which meant witnessing to Christ in words and deeds of love, striving for justice and peace, working for reconciliation, for pardon, healing, and liberation, everywhere.

Realizing that MRI was not proceeding as intended and that it had been "too largely identified with the Directory of Projects, and that this in turn led to a 'shopping list' mentality," the Anglican Consultative Council (ACC), meeting in Dublin in 1973 launched a program called "Partners in Mission."[12] This called for consultation in different parts of the world at which churches, with the assistance of representatives of other Anglican churches, would engage in self-study, planning, and the fixing of priorities. In 1977 the Episcopal Church held such consultations in all eight of its provinces. The experience was effective for a time, helping dioceses to recognize their resources as well as their need and to plan for the reinforcement of their strengths. The Executive

Council of the Episcopal Church received reports from the consultations at a meeting in Louisville, Kentucky, and said:

> We, the members of the Executive Council, have been privileged to share a renewed vision of Christian partnership. We are mindful that the mission of the Gospel begins, continues, and ends in God. The Spirit of the Lord has been moving among us at every level of the Church's life. For this we are deeply grateful.[13]

Although the program begun in 1977 was over-shadowed in the Episcopal Church for a time by another program called Venture in Mission (basically a fund-raising effort, highly organized and in terms of its goals eminently successful), there were positive results from Partners in Mission, to a degree represented by Venture in Mission itself. A major result was the further development of the companion diocese plan, which emphasized mutuality, with church members coming and going between the related dioceses, to their mutual enrichment. This plan, first developed by Bishop Brooke Mosley and called the Companion Diocese Plan, began in the 1950s and grew rapidly during the 1960s and 1970s.

The Church as Mission: The Theological Challenge

The essential challenge to the church to acknowledge its identity *as mission* began long before the Mutual Responsibility and Interdependence program was conceived. In a sense the challenge had always been there, for it was rooted and grounded in the New Testament and in the Hebrew Scriptures. A key moment of refocusing attention and altering an old understanding occurred at the beginning of our time-span, in 1952 at the World Missionary Conference held in Willingen, Germany. Some of the delegates attacked the motto of the conference ("The Missionary Obligation of the Church") and asserted that mission has its source not in the church but in the triune God: "Out of the depths of his love for us, the Father has sent forth his own beloved Son to reconcile all things to himself, that we and all men might, through the Spirit, be made one in him with the Father in that perfect love which is the very nature of God."[14] Regarded in this way, the mission is Christ's; the church is both the object of Christ's mission and its instrument. Indeed, instead of mission belonging to the church, the church as Christ's own body *is* mission. Mission constitutes its very being, for the church is the people of God gathered to be dispersed, witnessing to Christ and extending his mission of reconciliation throughout the world in all that they do and say where they are, wherever they are. In Emil Brunner's words, "The church lives by mission as a fire lives by burning."

The Anglican Consultative Council, successor to the office of Executive Officer of the Anglican Communion, held its first meeting at Limuru, Kenya, in 1971. Of the four working groups at this conference, "Mission and Evangelism" was chaired by Ralph Dean, Bishop of Cariboo and former Executive Officer. The secretary was Janani Luvum, then Bishop of Northern Uganda, later martyred at the hands of Idi Amin. The American representative to the committee was Marian Kelleran, the Vice-Chairman of the ACC and eventually its chairman. The question was asked: What is the church's mission? The committee reported this conclusion:

> The Christian mission is, as it has always been, the continuation of that explosion of new life, of faith, hope, and love, which was released into the world by the coming of the Lord Jesus Christ, his dying and rising, and the gift of his Spirit to men. We share in Christ's life as we share in the continuing of that mission.[15]

The report recognized that Christ's mission varies according to its contemporary context—although in essence it is unvarying. In 1971 the context included the conviction that God "is at work in the world, far beyond the boundaries of the church—in movements of liberation and humanization and in movements of radical renewal in the ancient religious systems." There was also an awareness of being human and of having that humanity challenged or denied "in the structures of our political, economic, and cultural life." Out of the context, thus understood, there came

> a recovery of biblical perspectives which had been forgotten; a vision of salvation as God's total, all embracing gift of healing and liberation for his whole creation; of this salvation being concerned with men's bodies as well as with their souls, with their corporate life as nations and societies as well as with their personal and private life; of the mission being God's mission rather than ours, and of its dimensions being greater than the creation and growth of churches.[16]

This statement directed attention anew to Roland Allen and the concept of indigenization (or adaptation) and eventually, realizing the defects of such terms, to "contextualization."[17]

Such a theological perspective also lent weight to concern for development in underdeveloped nations[18] and for alliances with human rights and liberation movements.

To some people the emphasis on mission as belonging to God, and extending beyond the church to all personal and social existences, seemed to de-emphasize the church's missionary work and to relieve Christians of responsibility for mission. Yet the ACC report did not arrive at such a conclusion. The work of the church "in preaching the gospel, baptizing and building up a visible fellowship" was viewed as "integral to the mission of God." From Pentecost on there was never a time when the proclamation of the Gospel was made "except from within a community of those who have become participants in Christ's death and resurrection." Then too, it was argued that the activities of the Holy Spirit can only become effective in history "through some institutional embodiment." The church was the necessary embodiment, but a fragile one, whose structures and activities may justly be criticized. The response to such criticism must not be an attempt to "escape from institutional forms, but must be a faithful endeavour to recover a common life centred in the given simplicities of the apostles' teaching and fellowship, the breaking of bread, and the prayers. It is these simplicities which give to the parish congregation its enduring place and significance in the Christian mission.[19] The church is of vital importance in God's mission and its missionary work (viewed in the broad context of the Gospel and of the world's needs) and is to be promoted, not diminished.

There was a tendency in the years following World War II to reduce the Episcopal Church's missionary work, in the name of indigenization, to renounce financial commitments and withdraw missionaries. In some places, such as in new nations from which all foreigners were expelled, such withdrawal was necessary. In other places the principle of indigenization seemed to be used as an excuse to divert funds and personnel to domestic programs. Furthermore, it was argued that the church's mission was not limited to foreign places. The mission was everywhere—and as a result for some it was in fact nowhere.

The ACC report echoed the conviction of many thoughtful people that the need for missionary effort and commitment was increased, not diminished, by the new theological insights. A fresh understanding was required, but the obligation remained. The obligation that does not change in the changing context, the report described in these words:

> The obligation to make known to all men the name of their Saviour, to invite them into a personal commitment to him, and to build them up as active members of his liberating fellowship remains an enduring obligation. But this must necessarily be in the context of full involvement in God's

contemporary work of liberation going beyond the boundaries of the Church, otherwise the work of evangelism becomes a distortion of the gospel. For the mission is God's mission; it concerns the whole of humanity and indeed the whole creation.[20]

It concerns not only such Christian presence as draws people into holy community, but also "the deliberate going beyond to those who are not, or cannot be, touched by the Church as it is. Such people can be touched only by those who are willing to risk losing themselves in another and alien community."[21]

The "new" understanding required that careful attention be paid to the relationship between evangelism and service, to mission and missions, to the necessity of making known the name of the Savior at home but also around the world, and to new ways of doing missionary work in accordance with MRI, Partners in Mission, the work of the Overseas Missionary Society, and the new voluntary societies arising at this time, such as the Episcopal South American Missionary Society and the Episcopal Church Missionary Community. David Birney, when Associate for Overseas Personnel and Scholarships of the Department of National and World Mission, identified the problem as one of apathy in the Episcopal Church and said: "Until the clergy and laity of this Church are once again committed to and given a vision of the world mission of this Church, in partnership with other Churches, I don't think we will begin to realize the great potential in human and material resources with which this Church has been blessed by God."[22] The vision required was one that involved a "new" understanding of the church, not as an optional institution of an optional God, but as a fellowship in the love of God whose mission is to be the constantly growing sphere of a constantly deepening reconciliation.

The 1980s saw a new thrust toward achievement of both a theological understanding of mission and commitment to doing mission at home and on a world-wide scale. The fifth meeting of

the Anglican Consultative Council in 1981 resulted in the creation of a continuing international Advisory Group on Mission Issues and Strategy (MISAG). It began work in 1982 reviewing
mission issues and strategy, identifying exceptional needs and
opportunities for mission and development which call for a
Communion-wide response, and finding ways and means for
collaboration with other Christian bodies in mission and evangelism. In 1982 the Standing Commission on World Mission of
the Episcopal Church published a special report called *Mission
in Global Perspective*, containing both a theological statement and
a description of the Episcopal Church's present policies and
programs concerning mission. This report served as a means of
wide discussion in the church and the production of a statement
of intention in 1985.[23] In September 1984 the Standing Commission on World Mission, the Diocese of Connecticut, and the Episcopal Church in Scotland held a Pan-Anglican Symposium on
Mission Theology. An interesting tension emerged in the course
of this conference, with papers presented by representatives
from all over the Anglican Communion. This tension, as the
editors of the book in which the papers appeared described it,
had to do with vertical and horizontal views of mission theology:

> The dominant view places most emphasis upon the
> horizontal dimension—on human relations within the
> world. The less-dominant view places more emphasis on
> the vertical dimension—on God's saving actions in the
> lives of individuals both through and within the fellowship
> of the Church.

> These contrasting views are not irreconcilable, each needing
the other.
> The way forward, we think, is suggested by Bishop
Caceres, who connects love, the Incarnation, service, and

the presence of the Spirit on the one hand with the passion of the Cross and discipline on the other.

Professors Philip Turner and Frank Sugeno conclude: "Our way we believe will be to find once again the connection between the Incarnation of God in Christ and the death of Christ upon the Cross."[24]

The necessary theological (and active) inclusiveness of the mission of the church was strongly asserted in the report MISAG presented at the sixth meeting of the Anglican Consultative Council in 1984, saying:

> There is a growing consensus that the Church's mission in some way involves proclamation, the common life of the Church, and the Church's relation to society as a whole. The mission of the Church involves speaking, being and doing. We can say that mission involves making known the truth about God revealed in Christ through what Christians say, through what they are and through what they do. Each must in some way be present if the words spoken and the deeds done are to have power. Thus if the Church only speaks of God but does not live a common life that shows forth the nature of God's life, her words will be empty. If the Church cares only for its own members and shows no compassion for human suffering and no outrage at injustice, the love she proclaims and displays will appear shallow and selfish. If on the other hand the Church only does good works and seeks justice she will fail to speak of God and so fail to make known the one in whose name she has been sent.[25]

The challenge to the ACC and the Standing Commission on World Mission of the Episcopal Church has been to engage the membership of the church at large in this discussion and to implement its implications for both the church in the United States and for global mission.

One effort in practical engagement was a program initiated by the Executive Council of the Episcopal Church and Presiding Bishop Allin called *The Next Step in Mission*. Congregations were called upon "to evaluate their life for total mission and ministry, endeavoring to increase their effectiveness through Service, Worship, Evangelism, Education, and Pastoral Care" during the next three years. Assistance was provided in doing this evaluation, with the expectation that it would result in an increase in commitment to mission in the broad sense. It was the kind of consciousness raising program in which it was difficult to assess results, but such an assessment was not uppermost in the minds of those who conducted the program. The results would be discernible in the future.

The Ecumenical Movement

The shrinking world gave impetus to another phenomenon of the twentieth century church, the ecumenical movement. In the years we have under review the Episcopal Church was a participating member of the National Council of Churches and the World Council of Churches, as it had been from their inception. There were church members critical of this involvement, including politically conservative persons who objected to the politically leftist tendencies of some conciliar actions. But on the whole participation in such councils and in local federations of churches provided much-needed assistance in areas where cooperation brought additional strength and motivating inspiration.

Two new ecumenical ventures were begun. In December 1960 Eugene Carson Blake, stated clerk of the United Presbyterian Church, preached a sermon in Grace Cathedral, San Francisco, calling for the reunion of divided Christianity and challenging the Episcopal Church to join with his denomination in seeking ways of achieving reunion. In May of 1961 the General Assembly of the United Presbyterian Church urged the Episcopal Church to join in inviting the Methodist Church and the United

Church of Christ to explore "the establishment of a united church truly catholic, truly reformed, and truly evangelical." The result was the formation of the Consultation on Church Union (COCU) at a planning meeting in October 1961, where the four original participants were joined by the Disciples of Christ and the Evangelical United Brethren.[26] Numerous meetings were held, the Chicago-Lambeth Quadrilateral was seriously considered in the ensuing discussions, and in 1970 "A Plan of Union for the Church of Christ Uniting" was placed before the churches for discussion and action. At this point the Episcopal Church came as close to organic union with other denominations as it ever had. But at that very moment the zeal for reunion through such an instrumentality as COCU apparently was waning.

Clearly denominational leaders were more committed to the COCU process than were the ordinary members of their churches. Denominationalism still had a strong appeal for many and the prevalent attitudes among Americans of privatization and individualization in religious matters were under-cutting efforts at reunion. The ecumenical movement was seen by some to be secondary to the crises facing the churches as a result of urban strife, movements for liberation, the Vietnam War, liturgical revision and women's ordination. Also questions were being asked about the value of such organic union—which would necessarily produce a giant bureaucracy. Stephen Bayne was one such church leader, a delegate of the Episcopal Church to COCU, who valued intercommunion above some forms of organic union, believing that one should first aim at intercommunion and allow organic unity to grow out of that. He therefore strove, as a delegate, to assure that the Church of Christ Uniting would emphasize intercommunion, guarantee the continuation of valuable diversities, and not take on the undesirable characteristics of a super-church.[27]

In fact great care was taken to avoid the dangers and pitfalls possible in COCU. As a recent document has stated, it was quickly apparent after the submission of the Plan of Union in 1970 that the churches involved "were not yet ready to enter immediately into full and organic union." It was clear also that they did not desire to put an end to COCU. "Hence, beginning in 1973, the Consultation entered upon a process of 'living our way toward unity,' through encouraging the development of Generating Communities, Interim Eucharistic Fellowships, and joint study and action. What the Consultation now refers to as 'covenanting' is a fuller development of that process."[28] Covenanting constitutes a step on the way to union, a means of "living our way toward union." It is "an act of solemn commitment to one another," and is "embodied in a process of identifying and taking certain mutually agreed actions which will move" the churches toward "becoming a visibly united church."[29] Covenanting involves striving toward theological consensus; mutual recognition of members, churches and ministries; and indeed various other elements identified with intercommunion. The process begun in the 1970s focuses on the church as a fellowship and upon the often difficult but ultimately necessary experience of reconciliation, rather than on institutional bureaucracy and coercive power.

The other new ecumenical venture concerned the Second Vatican Council and its effects on the Roman Catholic Church. A new day dawned as Geoffrey Fisher, Archbishop of Canterbury, met in 1960 with Pope John XXIII. Out of a meeting of Archbishop Ramsey with Pope Paul VI in 1966 there came the Anglican-Roman Catholic International Committee (ARCIC). Reconciliation was the theme of Ramsey's meeting with Pope Paul. In their *Common Declaration*, the two primates stated that "they wished to leave in the hands of the God of mercy all that in the past has been opposed to" the precept of charity expressed so clearly in Philippians 3:13–14: "Forgetting those things which are behind, and reaching forth unto those things which are before, I press towards the mark for the prize of the high calling of God in Jesus Christ."[30] ARCIC was the instrument for serious dialogue beginning in 1970. In 1971 there was issued a joint report on eucharistic doctrine, in 1973 a report on ministry and ordination, and in 1976 the first of two reports on authority in the church. The new atmosphere opened many doors and many hearts as members of the two long-divided churches began to worship together and to share responsibility in social action.

Once the hearts and doors were open some rather remarkable developments occurred on the local level, with enhanced cooperation between parishes: an exchange of ministers on special occasions and the joining of people at formal and informal eucharists. There were also instances in which the church hierarchies disciplined their people for moving too far, too fast. For instance, the relocation of Weston College, a theologate of the Society of Jesus, to the campus of the Episcopal Theological School in Cambridge, Massachusetts, brought about a committee for joint planning of worship and community life, a development soon stopped by the Roman Catholic hierarchy. Thereafter more caution was exercised, while there was still a strong sense of collegiality.

While the Episcopal Church remained in consultation with other Protestant bodies in COCU and with the Roman Catholic Church in ARCIC, other discussions were continuing with the Orthodox, Lutherans, the Reformed and with others. Union schemes were either beginning or already underway in various parts of the Anglican Communion, involving the churches of North India and of Pakistan, churches in Sri Lanka (Ceylon), the Church of England with the Methodist Church in Great Britain, and various churches of New Zealand. Also there were formal and informal discussions and negotiations occurring through the World Council of Churches. It became apparent that there needed to be some coordination of the various ecumenical dialogues, including some determination as to whether there was "inconsistency or even contradiction between the Agreed Statements" entered into with various church bodies. The ACC was to take major responsibility for such coordination and in 1981 noted the work already begun by the Faith and Order Commission of the World Council of Churches and the Secretaries of Christian World Communions in their Forum on Bilateral Dialogues.[31] Of great importance in this process of coordination was the work commencing in 1967 of the Faith and Order Commission with a provisional draft of ecumenical consensus on the eucharist, based on discussions at Lund (1952) and Montreal (1963). A first draft on baptism was produced in 1970 and one on ministry in 1972.[32] These drafts were much debated and refined until they emerged together at a meeting of Faith and Order Commission in Lima, Peru, in 1982, as *Baptism, Eucharist, and Ministry,* a troika of documents representing a broad consensus among more than 300 members of the World Council of Churches. It should be noted that the Faith and Order Commission included Roman Catholic theologians and others not members of the World Council. Though the final product had its beginnings in the 60s and 70s, the document on ministry involves an understanding of the church that is in agreement with that of John Knox, emphasizing fellowship in terms of communion and community, and reconciliation in terms of service and mission.[33]

The Ecumenical Movement and the Nature of the Church

The Anglican Consultative Council meeting in Limuru, Kenya, in 1971, confronted the question of the nature of the church and its mission, recognizing this question was fundamental to ecumenical discussions. New patterns of church life were expected to emerge. They "must be firmly rooted in the gospel of Christ and the Scriptures the Church has received," the Coucil argued, "but they must allow the Church to adjust its life, as a living organism to the pressure of a changing environment."[34]

There was much discussion in COCU of what the emerging united church should be like in relation to the church at large. Peter Day, an Episcopal layman and prominent leader in the ecumenical affairs of his church, suggested:

My thought is that we should see the uniting of the Church as a being and becoming one, a being and becoming holy, a being and becoming catholic, etc. And that all this is a participation in the glory that belongs to the Father and has been given to the Son and by him to those who belong to him "that they may be one even as we are one" (John 17:22).

One of the key words here is that of "participation," the church being constituted through participation in the glory belonging to the Father, given to the Son, and "by him to those who belong to him," the holy fellowship. In terms dear to Richard Hooker, Day thus pointed to the mystery of the church.

We find the same note struck in the ARCIC documents. In the introduction to *The Final Report* it is pointed out that the concept of *koinonia* (communion, fellowship) runs through the agreed statements. That introduction states:

Union with God in Christ Jesus through the Spirit is the heart of Christian *koinonia*. Among the various ways in which the term *koinonia* is used in different New Testament contexts, we concentrate on that which signifies a relation between persons resulting from their participation in one and the same reality (cf. 1 John 1.3). The Son of God has taken to himself our human nature, and he has sent upon us his Spirit, who makes us so truly members of the body of Christ that we too are able to call God 'Abba, Father' (Rom. 7.15; Gal. 4.6). Moreover, sharing in the same Holy Spirit, whereby we become members of the same body of Christ and adopted children of the same Father, we are also bound to one another in a completely new relationship. *Koinonia* with one another is entailed by our *koinonia* with God in Christ. This is the mystery of the Church.[36]

The specific agreed statements are redolent with this sense of ecclesial mystery and repeatedly refer to *koinonia* (fellowship) and reconciliation, reminding us of John Knox's way of speak-

ing of the church. Thus when presenting conclusions concerning
the eucharist, ARCIC stated:

> Through the life, death and resurrection of Jesus Christ
> God has reconciled men to himself, and in Christ he offers
> unity to all mankind. By his word God calls us into a new
> relationship with himself as our Father and with one
> another as his children—a relationship inaugurated by
> baptism into Christ through the Holy Spirit, nurtured and
> deepened through the eucharist, and expressed in a con-
> fession of one faith and a common life of loving service.[37]

In the statement on ministry and ordination ARCIC stated:
"All Christian ministry, whose purpose is always to build up the
community (*koinonia*), flows and takes its shape from Christ"—
his life and self-offering, the model of perfect service to God and
neighbor. "The Communion of man with God (and with each
other) requires their reconciliation. This reconciliation, accomplished by the death and resurrection of Jesus Christ, is being
realized in the Church's life through the responses of faith."[38]
The first statement on authority in the church, begins with: "The
confession of Christ as Lord is the heart of the Christian faith. To
him God has given all authority in heaven and on earth. As Lord
of the Church he bestows the Holy Spirit to create a community
of men with God and with one another. To bring this *koinonia* to
perfection is God's eternal purpose. The Church exists to serve
the fulfilment of this purpose when God will be all in all."[39]
The second statement on authority (1981) focuses on papal
primacy. It claims that while the term *jus divinum* need not be interpreted to mean that this universal primacy was founded by
Jesus himself, nor that papal primacy is the source of the church,
it can be understood to mean that the papacy is "the sign of the
visible *koinonia* God wills for the Church and an instrument
through which unity in diversity is realized. It is to a universal
primate thus envisaged within the collegiality of the bishops and

the *koinonia* of the whole Church that the qualification *jure divino* can be applied."[40]

The first ARCIC ended with this consideration of papal primacy, which was, perhaps, the least satisfactory of the agreed statements, especially in terms of the controversial matter of papal infallibility. There were other aspects of the agreed statements that were less than agreeable to many Anglicans. Mary Tanner speaks of "unresolved differences witnessed to in the texts—on the ordination of women and the teaching authority of the Bishop of Rome; there are puzzles contained in the Commission's own convergence—on the relation of ordained to lay ministry; and there are emerging related problems underlying the Commission's treatment of authority—Scripture and tradition, the significance of the closing of the Canon, and the need to articulate a fuller theology of episcopacy."[41] But there were gains, not the least being the theme of *koinonia*. Tanner states that underlying the picture of unity and diversity presented in the statements is the concept of *koinonia*. "*Koinonia* as both the goal and the way is far less limiting or static a concept than either organic union or conciliar fellowship. The riches and depths of *koinonia* will only be unfolded as the journey progresses with greater openness and commitment to one another."[42]

It is of interest to note that ARCIC II, which began its work at Venice in 1983, continued the *koinonia* theme in its first agreed statement, which is on justification and is called "Salvation and the Church." The introduction to this document speaks of fellowship and reconciliation. It begins: "The will of God, Father, Son, and Holy Spirit, is to reconcile to himself all that he has created and sustains, to set free the creation from its bondage to decay, and to draw all humanity into communion with himself." It speaks of the unmerited grace of God, the Holy Spirit uniting us with God and with one another in God. "This fellowship in one body, sustained through Word and Sacrament, is in the New Testament called *koinonia* (communion). '*Koinonia* with one another is entailed by our *koinonia* with God in Christ. This is the mystery of the Church' (ARCIC I, *The Final Report*, Introduction 5). The community of believers, united with Christ, gives praise and thanksgiving to God, celebrating the grace of Christ as they await his return in glory, when he will be all in all and will deliver to the Father a holy people."[43] It was apparent, in the ARCIC statements as in others, that unity in diversity was to be sought after and achieved through honest discussion of the nature of the church. In the course of centuries very different understandings had emerged, ranging from those influenced by concepts of universal primacy to those influenced by egalitarian and democratic ideals, from church to denominational to sectarian ecclesiologies. Furthermore the issue was seen as not only of concern among separated churches, but also within particular bodies of Christians, where diversity of understanding increasingly threatened their actual unity. Making the New Testament concept of *koinonia* a focus for the renewal of understanding provided one means for grappling with a most basic issue.

The Episcopal Church and Planet Earth

In and through all of these historical developments there was a slow but steady growth of sensitivity toward planet earth and ecological problems. There were some leaders in the Episcopal Church who saw this growth of sensitivity rising in relation to global issues in the United States and elsewhere. In 1972 *Limits to Growth* was published, the first report of the international Club of Rome, an organization founded by the Italian industrialist Aurelio Peccei. The Club of Rome from the outset had two objectives: "To promote and disseminate a more secure, in-depth understanding of mankind's predicament [and] to stimulate the adoption of new attitudes, policies, and institutions capable of redressing the present situation."[44] *Limits to Growth* made use of a computer simulation model of the earth developed at the Massachusetts Institute of Technology (MIT) by Episcopal layman, Jay Forrester, and refined by an international team under the direction of Dennis Meadows. The report, warning of dire results from unbridled growth trends, challenged a major economic and social principle of socio-technical society and stirred up a vigorous debate. The second report, *Mankind at the Turning Point* (1974), addressed possible solutions and called for a revolution in human values. It urged the development of world-conscious-ness, whereby individuals identify themselves more with global society than with national units, a new ethic whereby humans achieve greater satisfaction from saving or conserving than from spending and wasting, a new attitude toward nature whereby humans seek not the conquest of nature but cooperation with na-ture, and concern for future generations, that they may have suf-ficient resources to sustain them.[45]

In part reacting to the early reports of the Club of Rome, a group of scientists and theologians began meeting at the Epis-copal Divinity School in Cambridge, Massachusetts in 1974. It drew on such resources as seminars meeting at MIT, the work of the Boston Industrial Mission and Scott Paradise, scientists such as Everett Mendelsohn of Harvard and Joseph Weizenbaum of MIT, theologians such as John Skinner and John Snow, and theologian/activists such as Elizabeth and David Dodson Gray and theologian/literary critic Fontaine Maury Belford. The group readily identified the close connection between the "revolutionary" values listed in *Mankind at the Turning Point* and the teachings of the Christian gospel. In another report of the Club of Rome, *Goals for Mankind* (1977), the chief assets of Chris-tianity in relation to global crisis were identified, including "stay-ing power." It was contended that Christianity has staying power "as a universal religion, relevant to all men without distinction of nation, race, or caste." Furthermore, this report stressed, Chris-tianity possesses a strong ethic, one that is needed for the future of planet earth. This ethic was described in this way:

> To be at one with God is to have the mind of Christ, who went about doing good. The marks of the Kingdom of God are justice and mercy, forgiveness, sharing, self-sacrifice on

behalf of all who are in physical or spiritual need, and brotherhood with no distinctions of class or race. "By this shall all men know that ye are my disciples, if ye have love to one another."[46]

Through serious discussion, both idealistic and realistic, vision and understanding were shifting and developing among at least some of the church's members. One noteworthy event—largely ignored at the time—was the publication by a special study group of the Doctrine Commission of the Church of England, chaired by Hugh Montefiore, of a report dealing in terms of environmental and related concerns with global issues. The report was titled (in a way bound to offend feminists) *Man and Nature*. Here, moderns were depicted as raising serious questions only to evade them. For instance:

The population of the world is exploding.... Should we not do something about this? But why worry? If there is a disaster, it will strike the next generation and not ours....

We are using up non-renewable resources to the detriment of posterity. Should we not be doing something about this? But previous generations never worried about us. Science will find a way out of the difficulties....

We are overburdening our minds and bodies by increasing stress and tempo of life, with attendant stress illnesses. Ought we not to change our life-style? Yet statistically we are healthier than our forefathers....

We are dehumanizing life by the impersonal structures of modern society, by our addiction to socially destructive tools, by an obsession for consumer goods, many of them useless, unnecessary and even unwanted. Ought we not to be putting the needs of people and the cultivation of personal and communal relations before our insatiable desire for things? But mass-production methods are essential if goods are to be produced for all, and why should goods be produced unless the masses want them? If this is what the people want, then this is what they should have.[47]

The Doctrine Commission study group went on to suggest a new and relevant creed, thereby projecting a vision in tune with the Gospel and the crises of planet earth. It stated:

To accept God as Creator of all things implies that man's own creative activity should be in co-operation with the purposes of the Creator who has made all things good.

To accept man's sinfulness is to recognize the limitation of human goals and the uncertainty of human achievement.

To accept God as Savior is to work out our own salvation in union with him, and so to do our part in restoring and recreating what by our folly and frailty we have defaced or destroyed, and in helping come to birth those good possibilities of the creation that have not yet been realized....

To believe that man's true citizenship is in heaven and that his true destiny lies beyond space and time enables him both to be involved in this world and yet to have a measure of detachment from it that permits radical changes such as would scarcely be possible if all his hopes were centered on this world....[48]

The study concluded: "Only by the inspiration of such a vision is society likely to be able to re-order this world and to find the symbols to interpret man's place in it."

Here was a theology appropriate to the church and the world in the last half of the twentieth century. In relation to this theological perspective the church was appropriately viewed as a fellowship in the love of God whose mission is to be the constantly growing sphere of a constantly deepening reconciliation. Here was an indication of the church's mission into the future, far beyond the conversion of individuals and groups to denominations and churchly institutions. According to this theology the mission is to the world, in order to win people to the love of God, to bring them into a fellowship embodying God's love and to transform people from consumerism to sacrifice, from bombs to balm, from competition to cooperation, from fear to joy.

Not everyone was capable of drawing inspiration from such a vision as the Doctrine Commission study group presented. This was clear. There were still those who regarded such a vision as naive and utopian, urging instead the necessity of conflict and competition, perpetuating the escalation of the military build-up, and regarding the U.S.S.R. as "the evil empire." In such an atmosphere it was exceedingly difficult for the church to be the church. An additional counter-force was the tenacity of society's devotion to the principles of unlimited growth and unrestricted consumerism. To prophesy against such things was to expose oneself to the charge of treason and to risk being ostracized—going in the way of the Lord.

Chapter 4

Reflections on the Episcopal Church in Recent Years

A.M. Ramsey's Theological Reflections

In this brief study of the Episcopal Church we have been considering some of the major issues and developments against the background of post-industrial, socio-technical society with its understanding of the church as one institution among many. But we have also kept in mind the understanding of the church held by many of its leaders, grounded in biblical, theological, liturgical and ecumenical experience. The latter involves a vision of the church as the people of God (*laos tou theou*), the body of Christ of which Christ is the head, a sacred community indwelt by the Holy Spirit, realizing its true being through mission, Christ's mission of pardon, healing and liberation. The church is seen as a fellowship of fallible human beings, forgiven sinners, who struggle to resist the powers that work against the gospel (and thus against true humanity) but sometimes succumb to connivance in the distortion of the church and the destruction of its mission. The church is thus viewed as both holy and apostate, a potent power for good and an institution capable of destruction. As such it is constantly in need of renewal and reform in relation both to its origins in God the creator-redeemer and to its purpose as the instrument of God active in the present and into the future.

When Episcopalians urged, let the church be the church, they were pleading for a cleansing of the body and that it not be dismissed as "optional" by contemporary culture. In part, at least, we have been considering the church over against the individualization and privatization of religion in contemporary society, which denies the church's true nature as a fellowship (*koinonia*), and the tendency within the church to mirror contemporary society rather than represent the gospel. Such consideration and such pleading did not occur with or issue in a sense of hopelessness. Episcopalians on the whole believed sufficiently in the divine origins of the church to have faith that it would survive and live on, as it had done down through the centuries. What was the basis for such confidence? Michael Ramsey, in a thoughtful reflection on radical Christianity in the 1960s, looked back to the early church, the church of the New Testament and the apostolic age, and wrote in 1969:

> Christians believed that the Jesus whose history they cherished was alive in the midst of the Church and still teaching his people through the Holy Spirit and still feeding them with the Bread of Life. The life of Jesus in Palestine up to the Crucifixion was thus, in the mind of the Church, but one chapter in a continuing drama; and the stories about Jesus in the days of his flesh were now cherished as a part of a still continuing act. Therefore in the Church's use of the traditions about Jesus in Palestine, there might be a blurring of the distinction between past and present, between fact and interpretation.[1]

This sense of the living presence of Jesus was fundamental to the earliest Christians and basic to thoughtful Episcopalians in the recent past when the remembering of God's activity in and through the historical Jesus made the church aware of the living presence of its Lord. In a very lively sense Jesus was present in the critical years of the last half of the twentieth century through the community enlivened by the Spirit. That community was known to be his presence (the constantly growing sphere of a constantly deepening reconciliation) in and for the world, feeding the hungry, reconciling the alienated, empowering the powerless.

Liturgy as drama made Jesus' continuing presence and activity clear to many when such liturgy was vibrant with the gospel and of one piece with the ministry and mission of Christ. The faithful are gathered for renewal and refreshment and then sent out into their daily occupations to "love and serve the Lord" in the office, the laboratory, the home, the streets, wherever they find themselves to be as people of twentieth century society. J.A.T. Robinson wrote of "liturgy coming to life" in a Cambridge college and focused upon the Holy Communion —the "power-house, the hot-spot"—saying of the church: "I have insisted that liturgy, true and relevant worship, lies at the very heart of its evangelistic task, and that the Holy Communion is the creative centre of the whole life of the people of God. For it is here by partaking of Christ's Body, becoming bone of his bone and flesh of his flesh that we 'become what we are,' his Body in the world."[2]

If the church was to be the church, however, it was necessary that there be retained a clear sense of God in Jesus Christ immanent in the fellowship of disciples and yet separate, transcendent, not absorbed and thus diminished and distorted. It was necessary to view the church as simultaneously energized by the Holy Spirit within the fellowship *and* as under judgment, brought to repentance and renewed by the prophetic Spirit. God in Christ transcends the community not only in terms of the gospel, as found in Bible, creed, and liturgy, but also in relation to God's present activity in the world apart from the church, especially apart from the apostate church. It is God's activity in and through "hired razors," as well as in and through the poor and the oppressed who, in Matthew's telling of the gospel story represent Christ to the church.

The fact is, as Emil Brunner taught, that the church is not the kingdom of God. It is an agent of that kingdom, a fallible agent whose mission involves great risk, the risk of compromising its true nature.[3]Michael Ramsey wrote of the risk in relation to the doing of theology in the modern situation:

> The Church in its proclamation of Jesus as the Wisdom and the Word is called to follow the way of the Incarnation. It has used languages, images, analogies, and philosophies. The belief of the Church that the formulation of its doctrine has been by divine inspiration does not alter its recognition that all language is inadequate to the mystery of God in Christ. The task of interpreting its faith in a particular age and culture is beset by danger on either side.[4]

The archbishop, with events of the 60s in mind, described the dangers. On the one side there was the danger "of theology becoming assimilated to the world's wisdom in a false secularity." To avoid that danger it is necessary to cultivate and maintain that attitude of awe and dependency in relation to God that is at the heart of public worship and private devotions. "It is when we have lost the attitude of the worshipper," wrote Ramsey, "of awe and reverence in the presence of the Other, and when we have ceased to ask forgiveness of our sins," that we succumb to the absorption, distortion, and destruction in a false secularity. The other danger is equally serious. It is "the danger of theology becoming meaningless through not learning from the world which it sets out to teach." Here the archbishop spoke of the idolatries to which Christians are prone. He had in mind the church becoming so "religious" that it was blind to God's activity in everyday matters. He also had in mind that activism which leaves no room for the contemplation of God on whom all genuine Christian action depends. Idolatry arises too as Christians so absolutize their concepts and images of God that the concepts and images replace the reality they are meant to reveal.

What is the remedy? Ramsey wrote:

> The remedy for idolatry is the recovery of all the aspects of Faith as the New Testament writers present it. Faith includes assent to the pattern of things believed. It includes the recognition that God is. It includes the staking all upon an overwhelming probability to be tested by acceptance in action. It includes trust in God to act powerfully beyond our asking. It includes the attitude of one who sets out on a journey not knowing what the end will be. And it includes the trustful perseverance through the blackness of doubt, uncertainty, despair. Faith is not security away from darkness, it is the will to go on with darkness all around.[5]

Such theological reflection led to the realization that the authenticity of the Christian faith was located in the church at worship, living in constant communion with God, a fellowship of faith that is no stranger to doubt, the kind of doubt that attends all quests for truth and reality in contemporary society. Worship as it was viewed from A.G. Hebert to Massey Shepherd involved attitudes of awe and dependence, repentance and forgiveness, contrition and thanksgiving. It was not "other-worldly." To the contrary, it was understood that *litourgia* involves all of life. Franklin Young, an Episcopalian and New Testament scholar, wrote in 1963 of the New Testament attitude toward worship and demonstrated from the evidence in Scripture that, for the early Christian, *the* place of worship was not confined to a particular cultic center. The holy place was located "at the point where God confronts man in the person of the risen Lord (with respect to God's action) or the Church (with respect to response in faith)." Thus, as Young said, "the *holy place*, from God's side, is as omnipresent as the risen Christ (through the Holy Spirit); and, from man's side, it is co-extensive with the faith-response to God's act in Christ." He concluded, taking into account cult as well as place, that in the earliest times, "Worship meant responding to that total deed of Christ in one's total existence. Worship was understood not primarily from the standpoint of what man does, but from the standpoint of response to what Christ did and was continuing to do."[6]Thus it can be said that worship involves all of life—all places and all times—while particular places and times as necessary points of focus in order that all of life may be the obedient response to God's gracious action in Christ.[7]

Measuring the Episcopal Church against this understanding, as the church coped with issues of consequence both internally and externally, we realize that while it seemed to succeed in some ways and fail in others, still it persisted. The church was the church, while at the same time it needed to become what it was created and is recreated to be in the present age. This was so, the theologians argued, because the earthly institution was the body of Christ, empowered by the Holy Spirit.

Reflections on the Church and Humanity

The Episcopal Church from 1950 on was concerned for humanity and society at large. This central truth needs emphasis. The church in the midst of the crises of the time was demonstrating its commitment to the defense of human nature against all that threatened it, in the conviction that human beings as created by God are meant to be free in communion with God and with one another in God. The encroachment of modern technology, especially medical technology, on human freedom and dignity aroused discussion of the delicate balance between individuality and that sense of community we have been examining. The discussion had prompted Lambeth in 1948 to study the Christian doctrine of man and to warn against the dehumanizing effects of secularism. A report to Lambeth stated that Christianity "endorses every claim that can rightly be made for man"—having in mind individuals in particular. The report affirmed that in Christ, all humanity is ennobled, for He shows us what God intends man to be. All that makes for man's true fulfilment and enrichment is the friend of Christianity, all that thwarts or coarsens it is its enemy. This fundamental respect for human dignity, this vivid concern for all human decencies, which are the root of Christian civilization and are today so seriously endangered, spring from the central Christian dogma called the Incarnation.[8]

In the name of human freedom and dignity, the Lambeth report spoke of limitations to the "scientific" account of human existence. The sciences may be able to give adequate accounts of aspects of human nature, but they can never give a full or true account because the individual is always more than any scientific account. The human being "transcends the natural order, and no explanation of human life is valid if it is confined to naturalistic categories." The most important truth about the human being "is not his relation to the organic process but his capacity for the knowledge of God."[9]

This general understanding informed much of the succeeding discussion. Of particular importance were the reports of the Episcopal Church's Joint Commission on the Church in Human Affairs. In 1970, for instance, the Joint Commission's report dealt with (1) the ethics of medical technology, (2) moral issues of scientific technology, and (3) law, order and justice. More specifically, the commission was concerned with the impact of technology on life and death issues that affect individuals as well as society. Euthanasia, contraception, abortion, and artificial insemination were specifically treated. A fundamental consideration was that the "fulfillment of the humanness of man comes as he assumes the responsibility for the condition of his own situation and accepts or transcends these conditions. He comes closest to God, who recognizes limitations and works toward ways of pushing them back, who accepts the inevitable and transcends it, and who sees in the life process opportunity rather than defeat." The report concludes that it is

> the responsibility of society to provide for all men, of whatever station, economic level, ability, or talent, those opportunities for proper growth and development that will allow each man to exercise and celebrate his individuality within the community of man, to his and its corporate good.[10]

In a report submitted to General Convention in 1973, the Joint Commission wrestled with individuality, community, and their interrelationship, viewing the challenge of modern medical technology as especially threatening to the individual. Medical technology was viewed as overwhelming both technicians and the recipients of their labor with "a morass of facts, figures, and statistics." The result was "to remove from man both his appreciation of his real position in creation and his ability to determine the direction in which to turn for help, thus immobilizing him in decision making."[11]

In discussing such issues as euthanasia and abortion, the Joint Commission considered pertinent biological, social, psychological and theological data. It emphasized life as "God-given" and the family unit as "the proper place for the procreation and nurture of the new life." On the basis of the data the commission enumerated certain interrelated threads or concerns, for instance:

1. Human life begins with the genetic determination of the new individual, and continues throughout its development through the entire process of its death.
2. Human life is influenced by its surroundings and by participation in the decisions that affect it.
3. The free exercise of choice by every individual, with the knowledge of the alternatives open to him, and if pos-

sible the consequences of each of the alternatives, is
necessary for the full development of the potentialities
of each person.
4. There is a moral imperative to be actively, rather than pas-
sively, involved in the decisions that affect one's own life
and death....[12]

Such concerns and more (there were nine specified) were deter-
minative in the discussion of specific issues, such as contraception and family planning, about which the report said:
"Limitation of family size may be seen as a matter of conscience
by the husband and wife and should be so treated. Similarly, the
choice of the method of contraception should be handled in such
a way that the free exercise of conscience is permitted."[13] The
report was concerned with so called medical or health issues, but
the concerns listed pointed toward principles which were operative in the church's involvement in such social issues as civil
rights and women's liberation, for the Joint Commission was
concerned to defend human freedom and dignity as rooted in
the Incarnation.

A major obstacle to the realization of ideals such as those
enumerated by the Joint Commission was to be found in a per-
vasive, fatalistic sense of determinism in modern society. The
commission in 1970 recognized this fact and said, "If every stage
of [the history of the universe] is thought of as being inexorably
determined by laws of nature which admit no alternative or accidents, there is no room for either divine creativity or human
freedom. Man's moral behavior in such a world shares, in common with the number of his fingers or the size of his brain, the
character of being no more than the product of a machine-like
process."[14] To the minds of the commission members, such determinism was opposed to the gospel and to sound scientific theory.

There was another threat, emanating from what was in many
ways beneficial. The commission named this in saying:

A pressing question is the extent to which a computerized world will tend to rob man of his role of decision-maker, or at least to provide a path of least resistance to the delegation of his volitional and interpretive faculties to the machines he has made to serve him. In a world in which proliferating systems of communcation, with storage of personal data, become available to a variety of institutions and individuals, what unjustified invasions of privacy can occur?[15]

The very existence of a community dedicated to the protection of human rights, human freedom and dignity, and the necessity of human decision-making seemed to be in jeopardy. The promotion of a fellowship in the love of God required prophetic measures against all that threatened not only the church, but the very possibility of such fellowship (*koinonia*) as constituted the church—indeed, that threatened the survival of humanity as made in the image of God.

Reflections of a Seminary Dean

In 1976, toward the end of one era of crisis, a book was published in which the authors attempted to assess the position of the Episcopal Church in relation to major questions and issues then facing it. *Realities and Visions: The Church's Mission Today*, edited by Furman C. Stough and Urban T. Holmes, III, was commissioned by John Maury Allin, the Presiding Bishop, to assist in looking forward through the period of his term of office. In one of the essays, Urban (Terry) Holmes addressed an issue of great importance: the division between those who viewed the church's mission as that of providing comfort to its members and, on the contrary those who regarded it in terms of challenge. The bifurcation was between pastoral care and social action and as such it was seen by some as seriously endangering the overall mission of the Episcopal Church.

The stage had been set for the examination by Holmes, dean of the School of Theology at the University of the South, in the publication in January 1975 of the Hartford Appeal, a document sharply critical of the social activism of the churches. This was largely the work of Peter Berger and Richard Neuhaus. In January of 1976 a rejoinder was published, called Boston Affirmations, in defense of social action in and by the churches, written by Max Stackhouse, Constance Parvey, and others. The Hartford Appeal and Boston Affirmations dramatically represented the division afflicting not only the Episcopal Church, but all main-line churches in America.

Holmes rightly viewed the bifurcation as a modern phenomenon, a result of the peripheral nature of the church in the industrial west and the demise of the Constantinian church; the latter represented a situation in which church and state were in league on most matters. The social activists, seeing precedents from the Old Testament prophetic tradition, had been fearful of the emphasis on transcendence and of the church as a tool in the hands of the power-brokers—Christianity as the opiate of the people.

Dean Holmes found himself both appreciative and critical of the chief points made by both the Hartford Appeal and Boston Affirmations. He recognized that too often the church served the secular order, obscuring all radical judgment in its human pretensions and rendering impotent the freedom given in Christ. But he also knew that in the eyes of many, social activism was associated with riots, insensitivity to the ambiguity of motives, and a disregard for tradition. Social activism was seen as vulnerable to the seductions of secularism. Boston Affirmations contained simplistic statements, reflecting the tone of much modern secularism, statements concerning the perfect society, with the adulation of human potentials, enthusiasm for particular programs, and refusal to take account of the abject nature of all human institutions.

Holmes concentrated, however, on the Hartford Appeal, perhaps because he saw it as representative of the predominant mood in the Episcopal Church toward the end of the period of crisis. From the perspective of Boston Affirmations, the Hartford Appeal is wrong-headed, he said:

> It tends toward a gnostic dualism, which is more negative than positive, and it gives permission for persons to hide behind testimonies to the transcendence of God and life beyond the grave. The social activists have a reason to be apprehensive. There has been an unquestioned withdrawal in the Church from confrontation, sometimes by those very persons who were leading marches in the sixties. We are in the midst of a wave of pietism (the neo-Pentecostals, Faith Alive, the Cursillo movement), with its emphasis upon the emotional experience of God, inner reflection supported by small groups, and a kind of popular dualism of nature and supernature. The pietist tells us that what is wrong with the world is the corruption of the individual heart, perhaps adding that it results in the contamination of the material world. The solution is to "accept the Lord Jesus in your heart." This is obviously simplistic to a frightening degree.[16]

Holmes found fault with both documents, but also discovered important truth in each. With this in mind he urged that the Episcopal Church ignore neither one, but rather pursue the dialectic of comfort and challenge, pastoral care and social action, learning from the social sciences, for instance, without being seduced by their secularity. Thus he wrote:

> Contemporary learning is not opposed, as some suggest, to biblical insights. To use the latter to avoid the challenge of the former is to ignore the Holy Spirit speaking through tradition and reason, as any good Anglican believes it does. Tradition is a living thing, on which each age puts its mark.

It is not to be received and handed on as some inviolable package. Our times may not, as the Hartford Appeal suggests, be in possession of a definitive word, but certainly they have a potential for true insight as legitimate as the fourth, thirteenth, or sixteenth centuries.

Having said this, however, Holmes went on to argue that the church cannot, without considerable hurt and loss,

at the same time lose the vision of a transcendent God who creates, redeems, and sanctifies his world by being present and known within it and yet is infinitely more than this world. This belief in transcendence lies at the very heart of the Christian worldview. We can never settle for secularism or pantheism as a philosophy. While we believe that God created man with reason, and consequently is responsible for himself as embodied within a community and living out his history, we always insist that he work out his salvation under the vision of eternity. We become fully human by grace through faith.[17]

What Holmes meant by a dialectical theology he expressed when saying that "a dialectical theology would not allow a spiritual life to lapse into pietism any more than it would permit a concern for justice and human rights to become a mere secular program." The lack of such a theology resulted in both of these things, he said. "We have been asked to choose whether we are interested in prayer or social action, transcendence or immanence, tradition or relevance, orthodoxy or ethicalism, content or process, the Bible or psychology. It is time for the Episcopal Church to refuse to make any such choice and to live with the apparent contradictions embodied in the acceptance of mutually exclusive categories."[18]Such was a thoughtful man's opinion and hope.

A similar message had been conveyed twenty-five years earlier by H. Richard Niebuhr's *Christ and Culture* (1951), a book
which had considerable influence in the Episcopal Church. There
the Yale professor contrasted the three major positions with
regard to the Christian and the world. The first was that of complete opposition to the world: the world is regarded as fundamentally evil, and Christians pass through it as pilgrims on
their way to the heavenly Jerusalem. The second position was
that of complete acceptance of the world, whereby Christ is the
logical fulfillment of history and human institutions in their
development, looking to divine activity in the very secularities
of human culture. The third position, identified with Augustine
of Hippo, John Calvin, and F.D. Maurice, is "conversionist" with
regard to the world; it mediates between the first two. According to the "conversionist" position, "God is operative in history
and the church can be an instrument of his purposes for the conversion or transformation of the whole of life, personal and social (economic, political, and cultural). Here, Christ is the
'Transformer of Culture.' This approach rejects both simple ac-
commodation to the perversions of culture and mere repudiation, as totally depraved and corrupt, of the physical, the natural,
and the historical."[19]Emphasizing the possibility of conversion
or transformation, the third position was fundamentally positive
and involved, as indeed F.D. Maurice's theology involved, acceptance of both prayer *and* social action, transcendence *and* immanence, tradition *and* relevancy—for the conversionist point of
view regards the world and Christian ministry in the world with
prophetic insight. The world is the locale of God's continuing
creation and redemption.

The flight from social activism to personal piety that so disturbed Holmes led to a new era in the history of the Episcopal
Church, one in which we are still living. That flight was predi-
cated for some people on sincere convictions concerning the
gospel, for others it was a reaction to the excesses of social activists, and for still others the flight was a result of disillusion and

fear. Some of the most active members of the church became also the most seriously concerned as they experienced the rejection of their ideals and the failure of their movements. Some gave up hope, echoing Joseph Conrad's "deep-seated sense of fatality governing this man-inhabited world." The experiences of Americans in Vietnam, the bungling diplomacies of nations in possession of the means of self-destruction, the wavering economies—such things and more seemed to justify a sense of fatality and a turning from social activism to personal piety. The problem for the church was that implicit in this turning was implicit a denial of the gospel, which for Jesus involved pardon, healing, and liberation—not only for the sake of a few individuals, but for the sake of the entire world. The late seventies and the eighties were to be years in which the church continued to struggle with its self-understanding.

The Incarnation and the Church

In this chapter there has been reference on more than one occasion to the Incarnation. In 1977 there appeared in England a book, *The Myth of God Incarnate*,[20] that stirred up a controversy equal to that surrounding J.A.T. Robinson's *Honest to God* fifteen years earlier. As Michael Goulder, one of the contributors to the 1977 book, has said:

> It provoked hostile reviews in most of the religious and secular press; it was answered within six weeks by *The Truth of God Incarnate*, and later by *God Incarnate*; it sold thirty thousand copies in the first eight months, twenty-four thousand of them in Britain; and a call was made by the Church of England Evangelical Council (*Truth, error and discipline in the church*) for the five Anglican authors to resign.[21]

In part the notoriety of the book was connected with the prominence of its authors, including Maurice Wiles, Regius Professor of Divinity at Oxford and former chairman of the Church of England Doctrine Commission, and Dennis Nineham, who had been Regius Professor of Divinity at Cambridge. It was noteworthy when men of such stature indicated that the traditional doctrine of the Incarnation was no longer tenable, but was in fact dispensable.

The controversy did not have as serious an effect in the United States as in Britain, but it claimed the attention of the Episcopal Church especially when the Trinity Institute, under the sponsorship of Trinity Church, Wall Street, New York, made it the focus of a national conference. Major speakers were Don Cupitt, John Macquarrie, and Richard Norris, who objected that myth and truth are not necessarily opposed. "A myth, after all, is a story," Norris said. "It renders truth for us in a picture and so lets us grasp it imaginatively rather than abstractly; and at least in some circumstances that can be a manifest advantage."[22] G e o r g e Lindbeck, a prominent Lutheran theologian teaching at Yale, faulted the *Myth* authors for ignoring the "critical criteriological problem"—which has to do with the source of norms for identifying God. Is that source "the world of biblical narrative (understood as culminating in the stories about Jesus)," or is it "some other religious, intellectual, or cultural framework or language game?" He concluded, "If the former, then some form of postmodern 'orthodoxy' is the only alternative: the Christian God is defined by the Christian story. But this book takes the latter option. It tacitly seems to adopt the old liberal assumption that enlightened reason and conscience have access to independent or transcendent criteria which enable them to pick and choose what is of highest value from within the various religious traditions."[23]

Lindbeck's criticism is arguable, but his fundamental insight has been widely shared. Stephen Sykes, present Regius Professor of Divinity at Cambridge, placed the doctrine of the Incarnation in the context of the church, and wrote:

> To be an Anglican means to belong to a church in which the story of the incarnation is repeatedly rehearsed and implied, in its liturgies, including its most recent service books...the ethos of the Anglican communion is substantially determined by what is both explicitly professed and implicitly reinforced in its liturgical practice.[24]

For Sykes, as for others, the Incarnation was "an event in a story which renders who God is in concrete form. It is not a story which illustrates something which we otherwise already know, nor is it a story which is archetypal in the human consciousness. Rather it is a story whose meaning cannot be rendered otherwise than by the narration. It is, literally, indispensable."[25]

As an event in a story the Incarnation is presented and re-presented to us again and again. It is done in and through what Christians do when they assemble self-consciously in corporate worship. The story is interpreted in accordance with the present experience of the people of God and their remembrance of things past (and vision of things to come). There is not, as Norris reminds us, and there never has been a christology. There was certainly no one christology in the early church. "Christologies grow in and out of one another, whether by way of development or by way of conflict. They are individual moments in a long, changing tradition of interpretation."[26] Furthermore, our understanding of Christ affects the way we understand ourselves and our world, issuing in "new perspectives which in turn demand" we "change and deepen" our ways of appreciating Christ.[27] In one place Norris said:

> this person whom we call "Lord and Christ" is the one who establishes and actualizes what God is for us. Jesus is not merely a clue to what we might reasonably mean by "God";

he is the determination, the realization, of what God means by *us*. This is what is implied by all the New Testament's talk about our being "in Christ"....[28]

Stephen Sykes spoke of the congregation assembling for worship "in Christ."

That is not the same thing as saying that the church is the extension of the incarnation. Rather, the unique and unrepeatable incarnation of the Son of God becomes the basis of the text and of the offering in the liturgy, by the experience of the common contextualizing of diverse personal backgrounds and intentions in a jointly undertaken liturgical act. "In Christ" there is an experience of harmony and unity, such that in the liturgical act the community, in its fellowship with the whole body of the church, is a sacrament of Christ himself.[29]

The story forms the Christian and the community. Through the never-ending process of interpretation within the life of the community, the essential meaning of the story is realized not only in words (doctrinal statements) but in action (in the realization of the meaning in deeds of reconciliation). In terms of ecclesiology, the integral relationship of ecclesiology and christology was emphasized. The church is constituted in and through Jesus Christ, whose body it is, of whom Christ is the head. As the body of the incarnate one, the church is involved in the world while at the same time it serves as the instrument for the world's salvation. Involvement is a prime characteristic of incarnation, and the character of that incarnation is reconciling love, for the story informs us of who God is in concrete terms—God's humanity, God's humility. This in turn forms and reforms us in God's image, within the context of community, for service.

The Quest for Identity

The controversy concerning the Incarnation was an important part of the quest for identity during the late 1970s and into the

1980s. Undergoing many and great changes, the Episcopal Church needed to discover and own who she was under new circumstances. This is not to deny that the Episcopal Church is part of the one, holy, catholic, apostolic church, identified in the catechism of the new Prayer Book as "the community of the New Covenant." But as a church amongst churches in a pluralistic society, the Episcopal Church is constantly in quest of who and what it is—what its distinctive characteristics are, both negative and positive, and how it is seen in the contemporary world.

In 1978, prior to the meeting of the bishops of the Anglican Communion at Lambeth, there appeared a book by Stephen Sykes called *The Integrity of Anglicanism*. It pushed the question beyond one of identity to integrity, assuming that it is possible, through examination of official texts, to describe what is involved in being a member of one of the churches of the Anglican Communion. Sykes believed that the critical question is whether or not Anglicanism has a "coherent identity," and cited a committee of the 1948 Lambeth Conference which asked, "Is Anglicanism based on a sufficiently coherent form of authority to form the nucleus of a world-wide fellowship of Churches, or does its comprehensiveness conceal internal divisions which may cause disruption?"[30]

In quest of coherent identity (and thus of integrity) the Episcopal Church in the 1970s produced a new Church's Teaching Series, although this series was not related to the production of a new church school curriculum. The distance traveled by the church between 1950 and 1979 indicated the need for another set of books on the basic subjects of the church's beliefs and practices. The seven volumes published in 1979, "at the request of the Executive Council of the General Convention of the Episcopal Church" and with the support of the Presiding Bishop, John M. Allin, were framed by two volumes representing additions to the first series, beginning with a Christian apologetic, setting the stage for the volumes to come. The first volume, called *Christian Believing*, was written by Urban T. Holmes, III and John H.

Westerhoff, III. The second addressed Christian spirituality;
called *Living in the Spirit*, it was written by Rachel Hosmer and
Alan Jones, with assistance from John Westerhoff. The other
volumes were *The Bible for Today's Church* by Robert Bennett and
O.C. Edwards, *The Church in History* by John E. Booty, *Understanding the Faith of the Church* by Richard A. Norris, *Liturgy for
Living* by Charles P. Price and Louis Weil, and *The Christian Moral
Vision* by Earl H. Brill. Committees were assigned to each
volume, readability testing conducted, disagreements experienced and road blocks overcome. The aim, as Alan Jones of
the General Theological Seminary and chairman of the Church's
Teaching Series committee explained, was to speak "not so much
for the Episcopal Church as *to* it, and not to this Church only but
to Christians of other traditions, and to those who wait expec-
tantly at the edge of the Church." Nevertheless, he spoke of "a
definitive series of books setting forth the teachings of a particular denomination," realizing that this denomination is one in
which are found not only "a wide variety of opinions regarding
the substance of the teaching of the Church," but also "varying
and conflicting views with regard to the methods of com-
municating this teaching to others."[31] The volumes were in fact
aimed not at an examination of Anglican teachings, but at basic
Christian teaching on their different subjects. They were not as
easily read as the volumes in the first series, were written most-
ly by seminary professors, and reflected the latest critical scholarship. Richard Norris' *Understanding the Faith of the Church* was in
some ways the most successful; it provided an excellent brief survey of theology, and may have come close to providing the kind
of comprehensive theological discussion called for by Sykes.

In the same year another series was begun under the general
editorship of Theodore A. McConnell, called the Anglican
Studies Series. By 1985 there were seven volumes in the series:
What is Anglicanism? by Urban T. Holmes, III; *The Spirit of
Anglicanism* by William J. Wolf, John E. Booty, and Owen C.
Thomas; *Anglican Spirituality* edited by Professor Wolf; *The*

Anglican Moral Choice edited by Paul Elmen; *Anglicanism and the Bible* edited by Frederick H. Borsch; *Theology in Anglicanism* edited by Arthur A. Vogel; and *Anglican Theology and Pastoral Care* edited by James E. Griffiss. Contributing more directly to the quest for identity, these latter volumes tended to be more controversial, more representative of differing positions in the Episcopal Church and more interesting to read than the volumes in the new Church's Teaching Series.

The enterprise began with the Wolf, Booty, Thomas book entitled *The Spirit of Anglicanism*, inspired in part by Sykes' *Integrity of Anglicanism*. In his summary Wolf remarks of Anglicanism, "It is pragmatic in temper and greatly values common sense."[32]

Harvey Guthrie, in *Anglican Spirituality*, identifies three types of church—confessional, experiential, and pragmatic. The latter, which is the Anglican type,

> holds that what fundamentally makes one a part of the church is doing what the Church does liturgically, sacramentally and empirically. In the understanding of this type of church, the church is that body of people who have undergone baptism, who participate in the celebration of the Eucharist, who observe the Church's feasts, fasts, and ordinances. In the understanding of this type of church individuals may hold various confessional positions, may have undergone differing religious experiences or no particular religious experience at all. The basic thing they have in common is neither a doctrinal position nor a religious experience. It is simply participating in what the Church does as the Church.[33]

As to authority, for Sykes a key issue in Anglican identity, Richard Norris contends that "authority and order are resident primarily in a total structure, not in any single element within it. In that sense, they are quintessentially communal."[34] In *The Integrity of Anglicanism* Stephen Sykes viewed authority as dispersed. Referring to Lambeth 1948, he said that "authority is both singular, in that it derives from the mystery of the divine Trinity, and plural, in that it is distributed in numerous, organically related elements." Authority is dispersed, is "a mutually supporting, and mutually checking, life-process, in which the temptations to tyranny and the dangers of unhampered power can be resisted." Sykes went on to say:

> In respect of Anglicanism, the report (Lambeth 1948) claims...this authority is reflected in adherence to episcopacy as "the source and centre of our order" and the Book of Common Prayer. But it is significantly stated that the crucible in which these elements of authority are fused is liturgy, the offering and ordering of the public worship of God in the power of the Holy Spirit and in the presence of the risen and ascended Christ.[35]

The quality of dispersed authority was discerned to be closer to that of the good shepherd in John than to the imagery of Caesar's court or Reagan's White House. John Skinner, Professor of Theology at the Episcopal Divinity School, put it well when he said: "Authority must be contrasted to coercive power. Authority as nurture, anchored ultimately in the source of all reality, appears to be the proper meaning of the word. This conclusion occasions the following definition of authority: that kind of structured reality, whether social or personal, which through nurture and cultivation enables individuals to become truly centred selves or persons, and thus, relatively free beings."[36]

True authority, that is, true *exousia* is imbued with the character of humility (*tapeinos*).

In a sense the key word in Skinner's definition is nurture which stands over against coercive power and in contrast to conversion understood simplistically. The Episcopal Church at its best is a nurturing fellowship, in which people are fed and cared for and helped to grow into the fullness of the stature of Christ, which is true humanity, the end and purpose of human being. The law of such nurture is, as F.D. Maurice said, the law of our kind and gens, the law of kindness and gentleness, of sacrificial love.[37]

Chapter 5

Summing Up and Looking Forward

"Fellowship in the Love of God"

We have been considering the Episcopal Church in relation to John Knox's definition of the church, worked out in the midst of the crises of the 1960s. The church, said Knox, "is by definition a fellowship in the love of God, and its mission is to be the constantly growing sphere of a constantly deepening reconciliation."[1] In the first chapter we considered evidence supporting the notion that the church did indeed view itself as a fellowship, rather than as an institution, a corporation, or a rigid hierarchical structure that was fundamentally clerical and governed by canon law.

Such major concerns of the Episcopal Church in the 1950s and 60s as educational reform, with parish life conferences, group dynamics, inter-personal theories, and the Seabury series all seemed aimed at enhancing the church as a fellowship in the love of God. The liturgical movement and Prayer Book revision gained momentum from the 1950s, in agreement with the trend toward realizing the church as *koinonia*, maximizing participation in the liturgy by all people. The church was thus understood to be a worshipping community, or communities, and corporate worship was interpreted as "a vision of the People of God around the Word of God," the Word "proclaimed through sermon, scripture, and sacrament."[2] By the 1970s and 80s, and especially with the appearance of the 1979 *Book of Common Prayer*, the church was more and more regarded as a fellowship in which a people worshipping together in families were nurtured in faith, growing in knowledge and grace. John Westerhoff explained the close relationship between liturgy and learning, and the Diocese of Colorado provided a curriculum for all ages, which "brings together families and the church community in shared faith and worship. Using Scriptures appointed in the lectionary, lessons are geared to six age levels...and integrated with eucharistic worship."[3] The prospects of increasing predominance of technology in our society, the continuance of the "population explosion" and urbanization, and with no abeyance of the trend toward individualization and privatization of religion in America, indicated the vital importance of an understanding of the church as a fellowship in the love of God and a spreading and deepening of that understanding. This sense of urgency existed together with the further knowledge that to be human involves one in life-giving relationships with others, such communion and community that enhances our sense of individual worth. In our world the dignity and worth of human beings is constantly threatened by the dehumanizing and degrading trends of the corporation mentality, which issues in larger and more complex and dehumanizing systems. The church as a fellowship nurturing humanity is not only pastoral but prophetic, given the inhumane situation prevailing in our world.

The enhancement of the church as a fellowship in the love of God called for a radical change in the way in which all church people, ordained and lay, understood the church during the period we have been studying. In some ways the critical issue was that of ecclesiology, or the doctrine of the church. An important stage in developing the necessary changes in understanding began with the emergence of a movement dedicated to the "ministry of the laity." The key slogan was "the laity is the church."

Alden Drew Kelley emphasized this, as did others, including Hendrik Kraemer. Kelley wrote, "The laity is to be defined theologically by defining the church; not by contrast to the church regarded as clerics and monastics, nor as *part* of the church, nor as an *order* of the church. The laity *is* the church, period."[4] It was but a short step from there to the conclusion that clergy are servants of the laity. That was 1962; by 1972 the ramifications of this insight were apparent in a report to the House of Bishops on the ordination of women. At heart, it was said, the ministry is Christ's and through Christ belongs to the church, with ordained ministers representing both Christ and the church to one another and to the world as effective symbols of *the* ministry of Christ and the church. The church, then, is a sphere, as Knox suggested, rather than a pyramid hierarchically arranged, with archbishops at the top and common folk at the bottom. The sphere is the *laos tou theou*, the entire people of God, among whom there are various ministries to serve the mission and ministry of Christ in and through the church.

These ministries include those of bishops, priests, and deacons, servants of the servants of God. According to this viewpoint bishops, priests, and deacons, ordained and empowered to special ministries of leadership and service, are themselves laity, baptized, as Aiden Kavanaugh suggests, to priesthood.[5]

Fellowship (*koinonia*) is spherical, inclusive, holistic. The characteristic image is that of the congregation gathered for worship, the priest presiding, the people as a community being the celebrant, a "royal priesthood" gathered *around* the table, offering the sacrifice, offerings of their own life and work to be received back as the body and blood of Christ. Thus are the people fed by word and sacrament, nurtured in fellowship, growing in the fullness of Christ, into complete humanity. There humanity is acknowledged to be, whatever our individual condition, imbued with worth and dignity.

There is a struggle within the Christian churches amongst those who regard the church variously as confessional, experiential, or pragmatic. The confessional church demands of its members that they accept certain doctrines. Confessions such as those of Augsburg and Westminster come to mind. However there are also churches devoid of such formal confessional statements which instead insist upon their members holding certain narrowly defined doctrines, such as double predestination, or practices based upon doctrine such as the veneration of the blessed sacrament. The experiential church demands of its members that they have some form of religious experience, be born again, experience being baptised in the Spirit, or discern the truth of God's existence from experience, individual or social. The pragmatic church requires that its members participate in what the church does as the church. The Episcopal Church is basically a pragmatic church, as Harvey Guthrie says, "that body of people who have undergone baptism, who participate in the celebration of the Eucharist, who observe the Church's feasts, fasts, and ordinances."[6] In this context "believing is mainly belonging."[7]

Believing is not chiefly assent to propositions, but belonging to a community in which the story of God's dealing with the people of God (*laos tou theou*) is rehearsed in word and sacrament. The story is the story of the community, the story to which we belong. Doctrine is the interpretation of the story for the people living now, not a body of unchangeable doctrines but rather, as Richard Norris has said, "*a process of interpretation*"[8] in which contemporary philosophies, views of history, and understandings of the natural universe are used to aid in the process of interpretation. It must be stressed that this interpretation occurs within the fellowship, involves discussion, the *sensus fidelium* as expressed in liturgy and in bilateral discussions of the central, salvific story. In this pragmatic context, experience is fundamentally corporate rather than individual. Harvey Guthrie has said, "Anglican spirituality is corporate and liturgical and sacramental."[9] It is rooted in what we do together as the *laos tou theou*, in church as ministered to by word and sacraments and together in the fellowship (*koinonia*). The Holy Spirit is, in John

Taylor's own words, "the Go-Between God," who creates fellowship.[10] The Holy Spirit is active in the church and in each
member, beginning sacramentally with baptism, incorporating
them in the body which is the *laos tou theou*. In the corporate body
that prayer exists as "God's breath returning to its birth."[11]

It is in the context of the fellowship that, in Hooker's image,
angels descend with doctrine and angels ascend with prayer.
Personal religious experience, personal devotions, are roots; they
are grounded in the corporate, in the "fellowship in the love of
God."

I have noted that there is a struggle among churches that are
essential confessional or experiential or pragmatic. The struggle
goes on *within* churches, too. Although the Episcopal Church as
I observe it seems to be pragmatic, it includes those whose understandings of the church tend to be confessional and/or experiential, too. We have reason to ponder which of the three
understandings will predominate in the years ahead. I am concerned to state that Anglicanism (and thus the Episcopal Church)
is, and has been from the time of the Elizabethan Settlement in
1559, pragmatic. I would also argue that the pragmatic church is
the inclusive church, whose most pressing problem may be that
of setting boundaries. It is capable of accommodating diverse
kinds of Christians, confessional and experiential, but insists on
what Paul Avis has called "spiritual reticence," a high degree of
awe and humility in the presence of God, a reluctance to identify any human doctrine or experience with the ultimate will or
truth of God. Hooker, as Avis says, grounded ecclesial integrity
on the "outward profession of those things which spiritually ap-
pertain to the very essence of Christianity and are necessarily required in every particular Christian man, namely the baptismal
faith.[12] There is some reason to believe that the pragmatic tradition in the Episcopal Church is strong enough to restrain excesses in confessionalism and experientialism, but there is no
absolute guarantee that it will do so.

In part, its ability to do so will depend on its self-understanding as a fellowship in the love of God, a fellowship of mutual care and love, consisting basically of people (*laos tou theou*) nourished by word and sacrament. As such it is a people with special ministries serving its growth, its servanthood, the ordained ministers laity raised up from the community to special offices of service, service to the community, raised up as "faithful servants" of God's "Word and Sacraments."[13] Such an understanding is, however, incomplete unless the fellowship lives as a constantly growing sphere of a constantly deepening reconciliation.

"A Constantly Growing Sphere of a Constantly Deepening Reconciliation"

This image of the church is above all dynamic. It involves the development of fellowship in the ways we have considered—fellowship that is constantly expanding, reaching out, bringing more and more people into the orbit of its life and work, deepening that sense of unity in diversity and diversity in unity which is characteristic of the Holy Trinity and of Christ's body—the church as restored humanity. This understanding involves mission and ministry in a wholistic and vital sense; it involves reconciliation. Reconciliation is defined by John Macquarrie as "activity whereby the disorders of existence are healed, its imbalances redressed, its alienations bridged over."[14] Reconciliation involves the enabling of fellowship for the mission of reconciliation, the interaction (and even melding) of internal and external dimensions of church life.

In chapter 3 our focus was in part on reconciliation as mission and mission as reconciliation. There we witnessed how a seemingly revolutionary, fresh understanding of the Anglican Communion and its mission evolved, leading to the summer of 1963, at first in meetings held at Huron College in London, Ontario, and the Anglican Congress in Toronto, Canada. "Mutual Responsibility and Interdependence in the Body of Christ"[15]   was understood by Stephen Bayne, the man most responsible for it, to apply to the whole of the church's life and not only to "foreign missions," but to strife torn urban centers in the United States as well as to thriving churches in East Africa. Furthermore, there was in this concept no room for paternalism, racism, sexism, or narrow nationalism. Our unity in the one God speaks to the reality and the necessity of "mutual responsibility and interdependence" among all people. The church as restored humanity is meant to lead the way.

Thus, as we have seen in chapter 2, the Episcopal Church was called in and through specific events occurring in American society to live out "the gospel of reconciliation" (2 Cor. 5:19), which is to live into the saving story as we live into the secular culture we inhabit, agents for God's prophetic word to a broken and corrupt world. The Episcopal Church was called in the 1950s and 60s to combat racism in society and in the church, challenged by the Martin Luther Kings and the James Foremans to acknowledge its racist tendencies and commitments and to be reformed. Simultaneously it was called to engage in mission, Christ's mission to our society, to root out injustice and to assure that justice was done in the land.

Similarly, the church was called in the 1960s and 70s to combat sexism in society and in the church. It was challenged by NOW and by the women ordained at Philadelphia in 1974 to acknowledge its sexist biases and policies and to be reformed. The painful events were purgative and upbuilding, challenging to all. The question was whether or not the Episcopal Church could maintain fellowship at a time when the mission of reconciliation—which included the repudiation of racism and sexism—divided church members, alienated many church leaders, and in some ways lessened the effectiveness of the church's mission, turning its members inward. The charismatics and others disposed to renewal were right in observing that we needed the regeneration and reinvigoration of the fellowship in and by the Holy Spirit, both to maintain fellowship and to empower the people on mission in a deeply troubled society. The work of reconciliation still confronts us. Racism and sexism still exist in both society and church.

In particular, the Episcopal Church in the 1980s is faced with the unresolved issue of homosexuality in the church, especially the ordination of homosexual men and women. The gay rights movement of the 1970s, involving as it did the disclosure on the part of many Episcopalians—including some priests—of a homosexual preference, as well as the creation of "Integrity" as an organization advocating gay rights in the church, forced the Episcopal Church to react. The fact that there had always been homosexuals in the ordained ministry had been widely acknowledged, but ignored. Questions of whether homosexual activity was abnormal in God's sight, part of the sin of Onan, or homosexuals themselves rightly or wrongly ordained, became the basis of heated and as of yet unresolved debate. The General Convention cautiously allowed for the ordination of celibate homosexuals, while pastoral concern was expressed for all gay men and women, and ultimately the church turned out to be as divided over the issue as American society as a whole.

Gay Episcopalians had reason for optimism when Edmond L. Browning, an advocate of the rights of homosexuals, was elected Presiding Bishop in 1985. At the very least it was vital to recognize that gay women and men share in that dignity and respect due to all human beings as created in the image of God.

The issue in this decade is complicated by the onset and recognition of the Acquired Immune Deficiency Syndrome—AIDS. AIDS is a worldwide phenomenon affecting heterosexuals as well as homosexuals, recipients of blood transfusions, and drug users. In this country the disease is especially devasting to homosexual men. As many as a million and a half Americans are believed to be infected with the AIDS virus; by 1991, it is estimated, 179,000 will have died of the disease in this country alone. Doctors, lawyers, educators, entertainers, laborers, poets, musicians, rich and poor, young and old, men, women, and children alike are numbered among the thousands of AIDS victims who have died. This number includes clergy of many denominations, as well as the Episcopal Church.

The results of this death toll among gay men and women have been devastating. The Castro District of San Francisco, once vibrant with the sights and sounds of proud gay American culture, is now a somber and quiet place, a place of fear and grief. In San Francisco, New York, Philadelphia and increasingly elsewhere the Episcopal Church has established ministries to serve AIDS sufferers. Compassion is the most appropriate human and Christian response, yet unfortunately there are still many people—both within and without the church—who respond with fear and loathing. Issues of sexuality remain on the church's agenda of unfinished business. Where does the Episcopal Church stand on homosexuality and on the ordination of avowed homosexuals? It would seem that the church must acknowledge a wide range of views among its members, but whatever these views it is my conviction that they must be held within the context of the church's mission of reconciliation—not in the spirit of separation, segregation, and condemnation.

Nor have we solved the problem of war or eliminated the threat of nuclear holocaust. We observed in chapter 2 the tragedy of the Vietnam War and some of the ways by which the Episcopal Church responded to that war. Many of the church's members—politicians, theologians, foot soldiers and others—engaged in that war to stem the tide of Communist aggression, were patriots. But Cotesworth Pinkney Lewis was also a patriot. The dignified rector of Bruton Parish Church dared to put probing questions to President Johnson, questioning the wisdom and morality of the escalating conflict. "While pleading our loyalty—we ask humbly, Why?" he said. General Convention in 1967 declared, "War is madness. It is the scourge, the disease of all mankind. War is obsolete and if life is to continue on earth, all nations and all men must forthwith and without delay seek to accomplish its complete elimination, as an instrument of national policy."[16] The threat of nuclear war remains with us and seemingly will do so into the distant future. But at any moment it may come to an end in the death of planet earth or else in a new birth of commitment to God's plan of salvation through sacrificial love, which is at the heart of reconciliation.

In the statement by General Convention in 1967 the church's mission of reconciliation was acknowledged in words recalling the program of the Toronto 1963 Anglican Congress, "Mutual Responsibility and Interdependence in the Body of Christ." It said:

> We know that we are members one of another, and that in the face of our common extremity and the apocalyptic danger of our time, each man is responsible for all men, that what each man is or does makes a difference to the fate of all men, that all mankind will survive together or go under together.[17]

The point is deeply rooted in Anglicanism and brings to mind Richard Hooker's statement that "God hath created nothing simply for itself: but each thing in all things, and of every thing each part in other have such interest, that in the whole world nothing is found whereunto any thing created can say 'I need thee not.'"[18] It was John Donne, writing in the seventeenth century as Dean of St. Paul's Cathedral, London, who said:

> No man is an island, entire of itself; every man is a piece of the continent, a part of the main. If a clod be washed away by the sea, Europe is the less, as well as if a promontory were, as well as if a man of thy friend's or of thine own were: any man's death diminishes me, because I am involved in mankind, and therefore do not send to me to know for whom the bell tolls; it tolls for thee.[19]

In chapter 3 we considered at some length this awareness of global interdependence and encountered the challenge of the second report to the Club of Rome, to develop a world-consciousness whereby individuals identify themselves more with global society than with any particular national units.[20] The report of the Doctrine Commission of the Church of England, *Man and Nature* (1975), suggested the theological point in this emphasis, speaking of belief that our "true citizenship as Christians is in heaven,"[21] and that as citizens of heaven we are to work in cooperation with the purposes of God for all humankind and for planet earth, above and beyond any other considerations.

In the light of global understanding, the scandal of a divided Christianity is evident. Looking back it seems as though for every schism repaired at least one other has occurred. Yet there has been evidence of significant advance in reconciliation among the divided churches, including the birth and development of the World Council of Churches (together with national and local councils), with increased cooperation among the member churches, the new spirit of ecumenism in the Roman Catholic Church commencing with the second Vatican Council, and the Church of South India and similar organic reunions. The most striking evidence, however, may be seen in a developing new perspective, in part related to developments in ecclesiology. I refer to the prominence of *koinonia* (communion, fellowship) in the Anglican-Roman Catholic International Commission I *Final Report*.[22] It is in the context of *koinonia* that it is becoming more and more possible to understand the unity we seek in terms of unity in diversity, a pluralism with fellowship, an insight implicit in the COCU process of covenanting, explicitly addressed by John Macquarrie. Refering to expressions such as "covenanting," "conciliarity," "the concordat model," "a communion of communions," Macquarrie said:

> What all of these have in common is the recognition that the structures of unity must be such as to maintain in iden-

tifiable continuity with their past the several traditions that are to be brought together, so that there will neither be absorption of one group by another nor the levelling down of all in some new hybrid synthetic body.[23]

The *koinonia* way of reunion emphasizes fellowship. It aims at inter-communion, or table fellowship, without institutional mergers, although such mergers might in time result from living together in fellowship, a constantly growing sphere in a constantly deepening reconciliation. The sphere is one of unity in diversity, rather than monochromatic blurring, where reconciliation deepens as we learn day by day in countless numbers of ways to live together—to care for one another, to respect God-given differences, to enjoy creative variety, and to participate in Christ's mission and ministry together. As Macquarrie said:

> The need for difference within the unity of any great Church of the future arises not only from considerations about the nature of human communities, but also from the fact that the truth of God in Jesus Christ is never fully grasped from any one point of view.[24]

This insight points the way into the future.

The Centrality of the Incarnation

In chapter 4 we encountered what may have appeared to be a loosely joined collection of reflections on the church in general, and at times specifically on the Episcopal Church since 1950. There was, however, a theme and that theme was incarnation. A.M. Ramsey said, "The Church in its proclamation of Jesus as the Wisdom and the Word is called to follow the way of the Incarnation." Which is to say that although the fundamental Christian story is given, a matter of revelation, that story is always encountered as interpreted. Interpretation of the salvific story involves risks, for languages, images, and philosophies of any particular age are "inadequate to the mystery of God in Christ."[25] Yet mystery must be enfleshed and risks taken, not cockily but with a sense of awe and reverence in the presence of mystery and with humility, realizing that interpretations are ultimately inadequate. The doctrine of the Incarnation helps to save the church from becoming so "religious" that it is blind to God's activity in everyday life outside the church.

Incarnation was prominent in our considerations of the church and humanity. A report to Lambeth 1948 most clearly made the point. In Christ, it held, "all humanity is ennobled, for He shows us what God intends man to be. All that makes for man's true fulfillment and enrichment is the friend of Christianity, all that thwarts or coarsens it is its enemy." This statement leads to the conclusion that this "respect for human dignity," and "human decencies" ("the root of Christian civilization") "so seriously endangered...spring from the central Christian dogma called the Incarnation."[26] We have seen this conviction about humanity expressed in documents of the Episcopal Church's Joint Commission on the Church in Human Affairs, in relation to issues involving medical ethics and technology. The threat to basic human dignity of some advances in medical technology was noted, the commission having attacked "advances" that "remove from man both his appreciation of his real position in creation and his ability to determine the direction in which to turn for help, thus immobilizing him in decision making."[27]

Taking the Incarnation seriously involves Episcopalians in a) taking creation seriously, entering into the human scene, and b) striving to defend that creation against abuse, especially defending human beings who, in the light of the Incarnation, are endowed with human dignity and worth, no matter what their individual condition may be at any given moment. The nature of this incarnational view was expressed by Dean Holmes as he dealt with the conflict between the Hartford Appeal and Boston Affirmations, between comfort and challenge, between pastoral care and social action. Holmes recommended a dialectical theology involving transcendence and immanence, tradition and relevance, prayer and social action. Incarnational Christians are involved in this world, benefiting from contemporary learning as well as biblical insights. Their vision, however, is not wholly in and of the world but is "the vision of a transcendent God who creates, redeeems, and sanctifies his world by being present and known within it and yet is infinitely more than this world." Holmes put well this incarnational view, concluding, "We become fully human by grace through faith."[28]

Finally, there is the Incarnation and ecclesiology. Here it is perhaps sufficient to note that out of the controversy over the doctrine of the Incarnation, sparked by the appearance of *The Myth of God Incarnate* (1977), came the statement of Stephen Sykes concerning the centrality of the Incarnation as the foundation of the church. The people assemble for worship, "in Christ." This was not to say, Sykes claimed, that the church is the extension of the Incarnation. "Rather, the unique and unrepeatable incarnation of the Son of God becomes the basis of the text and of the offering in the liturgy...'in Christ' there is an experience of harmony and unity, such that in the liturgical act of the community, in its fellowship with the whole body of the church, is a sacrament of Christ himself."[29]

Such an understanding conforms well to the pragmatic understanding of the church as expressed by Harvey Guthrie,[30] and to the identity—through word and sacrament—of the Episcopal Church as a fellowship for which authority is chiefly nurturing, through nurture enabling individuals "to become truly centered selves or persons."[31]

Richard Hooker and Anglican Tradition

In conclusion, it is evident to me that in the midst of the crises, the Episcopal Church was struggling to realize in thought and in action the true nature of the church as a fellowship in the love of

God. It was responding to the demand that the church be the church and not a mere reflection of the society in which it dwelt and to which it was sent with the gospel. As I look back upon this struggle I think of Richard Hooker and Anglican tradition as it is associated with him and his theological understanding of the church and its mission. That understanding, made clearer in recent years as a result of a new and critical edition begun in 1969 of his *Works*, is grounded in the conviction that the church is a fellowship of people distinguished by their "participation" in Christ—that was a favorite expression of his—for the sake of Christ's ministry of reconciliation in a troubled and broken world.

For Hooker, salvation involved reconciliation with God and with one another in God—that is, in the fellowship, the mutual participation of the Holy Trinity. Salvation concerned participation (*koinonia; meno, menein*) in Christ which is at one and the same time "incorporation into that society which hath him for their Lord and doth make together with him one body...for which cause by virtue of this mystical conjunction we are of him and in him [Eph. 5:30] as though our very flesh and bones should be made continuate with his."[32] Thus the church is the body of Christ formed by God "out of the flesh, the very wounded and bleeding side of the Son of man. His body crucified and his blood shed for the life of the world, are the true elements of that heavenly being, which maketh us [1 Cor. 15:48] such as him self of whom we come" (V.56.7).

In this definition of the church there is an awareness of the sacredness of the fellowship, not as a powerful institution, but as the very flesh and blood of Christ. The church is holy, but not proud. As the body of Christ it was founded for service, service qualified by humility. The church is sacred, for in and through it the members partake of Christ, are fed by his sacraments, nourished by the gospel, enjoy a healing, life-giving fellowship, and are in Christ as he is in them. The importance of stating and restating the belief that the church is Christ's body was emphasized by Robert Isaac Wilberforce, the friend of Newman and theologian of the early Tractarians. He went so far as to say that the errors of the church in modern society "result from a forget-fulness of the central truth, that the Church of Christ is His Body; His Presence is its life; its blessing the gift of spiritual union with His man's nature."[33] The great error is to revere the church and not Christ, failing to regard the church as Christ's own body.

The church is the body of Christ, the body of the Servant Lord, engaged in his ministry and mission in the present age. The church is, therefore, "one body" (Eph. 2:16; III.1.3.). Its unity con-sists in its identity with "one Lord" whom it professes, "one faith" which its members acknowledge, and "one baptism wherewith they are all initiated" (Eph. 4:5; III.1.3). This unity Hooker elo-quently described, saying:

> They which belong to the mystical body of our Savior Christ and be in number as the stars of heaven, divided suc-cessively by reason of their mortal condition into many generations, are notwithstanding coupled every one to Christ their head and all unto every particular person amongst them selves, in as much as the same Spirit, which annointed the blessed soul of our Savior Christ, doth so for-malize unite and actuate his whole race, as if both he and they were so many limbs compacted into one body, by being quickened all with one and the same soul (V.56.11).

This basic unity acknowledged, Hooker spoke of diversity within the unity. It is a diversity of graces given and graces received, diversity of perfection in grace and in righteousness, diversity of calls and vocations. "Diversity in unity" may justly be considered a major principle of Hooker's ecclesiology, derived from serious reflection on the New Testament and the early church fathers, as well as on the church of his day. To the degree that he acknowledged diversity Hooker ran counter to the anxious quest for uniformity on the part of many in the sixteenth century, especially the Puritans against whom he wrote, as well as members of the ecclesiastical establishment whose views he otherwise shared and defended.

Another of Hooker's principles was a consistent concern for detecting the purpose or end for anything and everything; this was his teleological principle, derived from Aristotle, and Thomas Aquinas. It seems clear that the purpose of the church, on at least one level, was the reconciliation of all creation with God in Christ. One might say, as some Anglicans after Hooker did, that the church *is* reconciled, redeemed humanity. The church is the world, often fragmented and separated from God, consciously acknowledging in word and deed the mutual participation which it enjoys in God. The sacraments are given for the perfection of the world. Baptism and the Holy Communion are instrumental causes for that participation in Christ whereby "such effects as being derived from both natures of Christ... are made our own." They convey "a true actual influence of grace whereby the life which we live according to godliness is his, and from him we receive those perfections wherein our eternal happiness consisteth" (V.67.5). The church thus was not founded to serve itself, but to give its life in service to others and provide for the true happiness of humanity, created by God in love for love. Nourished by the sacraments, Christians are ever more deeply in union with Christ and on mission with him, the mission of sacrificial service. Such, I believe, is the thrust of Hooker's teaching. Essential to it was a fixed attention on the purpose for which the church exists—on Christ and his ministry and mission in and for the world.

Participation, mutual participation—here is another fundamental principle and it is one with serious implications. The principle of participation stands opposed to self-serving individualism in both religion and politics and all of life. It supports the view of F.D. Maurice that cooperation is always preferable to competition, not on the basis of some sentimental urge but rather of his understanding that the principle ruling the universe is sacrifice. Participation in Hooker's teaching requires mutual sacrifice, sharing, cooperation, and self-forgetful love. And the principle of participation challenges pride (*hubris*) and all that separates us from God and from one another in God. Hooker put his case simply in his sermon on pride: "God hath created nothing simply for itself: but each thing in all things, and of everything each part in other have such interest, that in the whole world nothing is found whereunto any thing created can say, 'I need thee not.'"[34]

Furthermore, in his concern for the universe of laws as expressed in Books I and V of the *Laws*, Hooker tended to reject the arbitrary exercise of power whether that of the monarch or of bishops. This was not to deny due authority to either, but to acknowledge that neither was above the law in the universe of laws. It is possible to go further than this, however. In a careful examination of Book VIII of the *Laws*, in relation to newly discovered draft notes made by Hooker as he prepared to write on royal supremacy, A.S. McGrade has concluded that Hooker emphasized the whole community—not king alone, not bishops alone, and not king and bishops alone—as "the source of coercive authority in all matters."[35] McGrade writes: "The strength of Hooker's position...lies in its capacity for including all parts of a community in legislative decisions concerning the community and in insisting that the crown...should operate in accordance with those communal decisions."[36]

Reflecting on this affirmation by Hooker of the authority of the community with respect to both church and state, it is possible, I believe, to discover another principle, which is that the church is the whole people. It is not the clergy alone, nor the *laos* from which the clergy are subtracted. For good or ill, the guidelines or laws by which the church governs its life and pursues its mission are the responsibility of the whole church through representative agents, agents that truly strive to represent the people and do not forget who made them agents. If the church is the body of Christ and the body of Christ is the entire *laos* and not some part of it, then it is requisite that the over-arching authority of the whole be recognized, not grudgingly but sincerely in faith, respecting the operation of the Spirit in the midst of the people, thus allowing Christ to rule his body.

The principle should be seen, of course, in relation to what Hooker regarded as essential: one Lord, one faith, one baptism. But here caution must be exercised. For Hooker the authority whereby we are governed—maintained in the essentials—is not to be restricted to Scripture or tradition or reason. Each presupposes the operation of the others. Nor is it right to restrict our attention to the doctrinal three-legged stool, although normatively for Anglicanism authority for doctrine involves Scripture, tradition, and reason interrelated and in creative tension with one another. It is not enough to add a fourth leg—experience—as many Anglicans do, influenced by scientific empiricism and other trends of our society. Hooker, in rejecting the over-emphasis on the authority of Scripture made by Puritans, wrote:

> Whatsoever either men on earth, or the Angels of heaven do know; it is as a drop of that unemptiable fountain of wisdom, which wisdom hath diversely imparted her treasures into the world. As her ways are of sundry kinds, so her manner of teaching is not merely one and the same. Some things she openeth by the sacred books of Scripture; some things by the glorious works of nature: with some things she inspireth them from above by spiritual influence, in some things she leadeth and traineth them only by worldly experience and practise. We may not so in any one special kind admire her that we disgrace her in any other, but let all her ways be according unto their place and degree adored (II. 1.4).[37]

The church as a decision-making community is informed through the many ways by which God communicates with its members. The church properly speaking lives in awe. It is open to the working of God's Spirit in expected and unexpected ways, tolerant of those in the community who deviate from recognized norms, firm in its unity in one Lord, one faith, one baptism. The church, ideally speaking, is people conferring with one another, speaking the truth in love, while making decisions, sometimes difficult and often painful decisions, but *making decisions*, confessing, as they decide that they are fallible, sinful people, *in via* and not yet *in patria*, in need of reform and renewal, praying that they may be obedient servants of their Lord.

The process of communal decision-making was sorely tried in the Episcopal Church between 1950 and the 1980s. The process was painful for most people—devastatingly painful—and it was seriously harmful for some. But the process was essential, whatever the cost. To take but one example, consider the process of liturgical revision. It is widely understood that Prayer Book revision is a critical occupation for Anglicanism, in which the Prayer Book provides the context for doing theology and reaching theological consensus. It is the basis for teaching the necessary faith in relation to life-issues and maintaining the church as a whole in the unity of one Lord, one faith, one baptism. The process pursued involved years of study by the Standing Liturgical Commission of General Convention, followed by the drafting and dissemination of trial liturgies, including the 1967 Eucharist, the Green Book, The Zebra Book, and the Proposed Book. They solicited in formal and informal ways opinions from all dioceses and, through the dioceses, from all parishes and missions, with final decisions made in two General Conventions. In the midst of this process, concern was expressed time and again that the authority of Scripture, tradition, and reason—as well as experience—be respected. In addition, pains were taken to counsel with other churches of the Anglican Communion and with those churches beyond Anglicanism with which the Episcopal Church was involved ecumenically. The resulting 1979 *Book of Common Prayer* was influenced by thousands of people. It did not satisfy everyone, and it could not do so, given the wide diversity within the unity we have. But it provided for the needs of a wide spectrum of Episcopalians. Nor is there any sense of having arrived at the end of the process. The 1979 Prayer Book is incomplete, pointing toward the need for further revision, encouraging a continuing discussion within the church as to the nature of its unity in one Lord, one faith, one baptism.

The success of such a process depends on the ability of the *laos* to recognize its responsibility. That in turn depends on the ability and willingness on the part of everyone to perceive the church as the entire community, the body of Christ. Such recognition and perception is not easily achieved in contemporary society, but it is vitally important both to the church and to society at large. The church as the entire community of Christians in any given place, living and growing as the body of Christ, exists for reconciliation not only in the church, but also in the world to which the church is sent with the gospel of reconciliation.

Pray God that the church may be the church—a fellowship in the love of God whose mission is to be the constantly growing sphere of a constantly deepening reconciliation.

NOTES

Introduction

1. *The New York Times Magazine,* July 25, 1986, p. 20.
2. Stephen Sykes, *The Identity of Christianity* (London: SPCK, 1984), p. 3.
3. Ibid., pp. 26–27.

Chapter 1

1. In William Stringfellow and Anthony Towne, *The Bishop Pike Affair* (New York: Harper and Row, 1967), p. 220.
2. Ibid., p. 223.
3. *Theological Freedom and Responsibility.* Report of the Advisory Committee of the Episcopal Church (New York: Seabury, 1967), pp. 67–68.
4. Ibid., p. 70.
5. Henri de Lubac, cited in Avery Dulles, *Models of the Church* (Garden City, N.Y.: Image Books, Doubleday and Company, 1978), p. 67, from *Catholicism* (London, 1950), p. 29.
6. *Theological Freedom,* p. 70.
7. See Joachim Wach, *Sociology of Religion* (Chicago: University of Chicago Press, 1944).
8. Cited by John Skinner, *The Meaning of Authority* (Washington, D.C.: The University Press of America, 1983), p. 7.
9. Langdon Gilkey, *Naming the Whirlwind: The Renewal of God-Language* (Indianapolis and New York: Bobbs-Merrill Company, 1969), p. 24.

10. Joseph Fletcher, *Situation Ethics: The New Morality* (Philadelphia: The Westminster Press, 1966), p. 158.

11. See Seward Hiltner, "A Descriptive Appraisal, 1935–1980," *Pastoral Psychology*, Winter 1960, pp. 86–98, and Richard Dayninger, "Goals in Clinical Pastoral Education," *Pastoral Psychology*, April 1971, pp. 5–10.

12. In R.E. Tirwilliger and U.T. Holmes, III, eds. *To Be a Priest* (New York: Seabury, 1975), pp. 176–77.

13. See Eli Wismer, "Small Groups and Church Renewal," *Pastoral Psychology*, March 1967, pp. 7–13.

14. Quoted in John Booty, "Since the Reformation: An Emphasis on the American Experience," J.H. Westerhoff, III, and O.C. Edwards, Jr., eds., *The Faithful Church: Issues in the History of Catechesis* (Wilton, Ct.: Morehouse-Barlow, 1984), p. 284.

15. See George E. DeMille, *The Episcopal Church Since 1900: A Brief History* (New York: Morehouse-Gorham Company, 1955), pp. 124–28.

16. See Philip H. Phenix, *Education and the Worship of God* (Philadelphia: The Westminster Press, 1966).

17. See Charles P. Price, *Introducing the Proposed Book of Common Prayer* (New York: Seabury, 1977), pp. 10–12.

18. In *The Honest to God Debate*, David L. Edwards, ed. (Philadelphia: The Westminster Press, 1963), p. 18.

19. See John Booty, *The Godly Kingdom of Tudor England* (Wilton, Ct.: Morehouse-Barlow, 1981), esp. the Introduction and Chapter 2.

20. Horton Davies, *Worship and Theology in England*, v. 5 (Princeton: Princeton University Press, 1965), p. 40.

21. See esp. Hooker, *Laws*, Book V, chapters 56, 57, 67.

22. S.F. Bayne, Jr., "What the Proposed Liturgy Should Proclaim," *St. Luke's Journal of Theology*, v. 12, May 1969, p. 24.

23. In *A Faithful Church*, Westerhoff and Edwards, eds., p. 296.

24. Ibid., p. 307.

25. See James B. Fowler, *Stages of Faith* (San Francisco: Harper and Row, 1981) and for an interesting summary Ruth Tiffany

Barnhouse "Secular and Religious Models of Care," *Anglican Theology and Pastoral Care*, J.E. Griffiss ed. (Wilton, Ct.: Morehouse-Barlow, 1985), pp. 62– 63.

26. *The Episcopalian*, May, 1980.

27. T.O. Wedel, *The Gospel in a Strange, New World* (Philadelphia: The Westminster Press, 1963), pp. 96– 97.

28. Alden D. Kelley, *The People of God: A Study in the Doctrine of the Laity* (Greenwich: Seabury, 1962), pp. 11, 33.

29. John Macquarrie, *Principles of Christian Theology* (New York: Scribner's, 1966), p. 374.

30. Robert Grant, "Christian Ministry and the People of God," *Today's Church and Today's World*, Lambeth 1978 (London: CIO, 1977), p. 168.

31. Macquarrie, *Principles*, p. 374.

32. Henrik Kraemer, *A Theology of the Laity* (London: Lutterworth, 1958), pp. 139–140.

33. Kelley, *People of God*, p. 32.

34. J.A.T. Robinson, "The Ministry of the Laity," *Layman's Church* (London: Lutterworth, 1963), p. 17.

35. F.O. Ayres, *The Ministry of the Laity: A Biblical Exposition* (Philadelphia: The Westminster Press, 1962), p. 15.

36. Ibid., p. 19.

37. In *Ministry Development Journal*, Spring 1983, p. 29.

38. Kelley, *People of God*, p. 13.

39. Robinson, "Ministry," p. 17.

40. Ibid., p. 18.

41. House of Bishops, document 72165, p. 2.

42. See, for instance, *Deacons in the Liturgy*, by Ormonde Plater (1981), *The Diaconate: A Full and Equal Order*, by James M. Barnett (1981), and *The Servant Church: Diaconal Ministry and the Episcopal Church*, by John Booty (1982).

43. House of Bishops, document 72165, p. 3.

44. Ibid. See Trinity Institute, *Toward a Theology of Priesthood* (New York, 1982).

45. House of Bishops, document 72165, p. 4.

46. Booty, *Servant Church*, p. 61.

47. Pike and Pittenger, *The Faith of the Church*, pp. 137–38.

48. In Kelley, *People of God*, p. 24.

49. Richard Norris, "The People of Grace," *Theology in Anglicanism*, Arthur A. Vogel, ed. (Wilton, Ct.: Morehouse- Barlow, 1984), pp. 106–07.

50. Ibid., 107.

51. *Towards a Theology of Priesthood*, Trinity Institute (1982), p. 2.

52. Norris, "People of Grace," p. 109.

53. Charles R. Feilding, *Education for Ministry* (Dayton, Ohio: American Association of Theological Schools, 1966), p. 10.

54. *Ministry for Tomorrow*. Report of the Special Committee on Theological Education (New York: Seabury, 1967), p. ix.

55. Ibid., p. 120.

56. Ibid.

57. Ibid., p. 128.

58. SFB to all bishops, January 11, 1971, Bayne Archives, drawer #3, 40c.

59. See GBEC Minutes, October 14–16, 1971, and "Interim Report to the House of Bishops," October 24, 1971.

60. Farley, *Theologia* (Philadelphia: Fortress Press, 1983), see esp. ch. 7.

61. *Journal of General Convention*, 1967, pp. 1ff.

Chapter 2

1. Langdon Winner, *The Whale and the Reactor: A Search for Limits in an Age of High Technology* (Chicago: University of Chicago Press, 1986), p. 50.

2. See Richard Shickel, *Intimate Strangers: The Culture of Celebrity* (Garden City, New York: Doubleday and Company, 1985).

3. William H. Chafe, *The Unfinished Journey: America Since World War II.* (New York: Oxford University Press, 1986), p. 121.

4. William Clark Roof, "America's Voluntary Establishment: Mainline Religion in Transition," *Daedalus*, vol. 3, no. 1, Winter

1982, pp. 166–67; see also Martin E. Marty, "Religion in America Since Mid-Century," ibid., pp. 149–63.

5. Samuel P. Huntington, *American Politics: The Promise of Disharmony* (Cambridge: Mass.: The Belknap Press of Harvard University Press, 1981), p. 2.

6. See Chafe, *Unfinished Journey*, p. 21. These riots in the summer of 1943 marked a turning point. "To many," wrote Chafe, "the Detroit race riots symbolized not only the rawness of race relations in America, but also a new spirit of militancy and assertiveness among American blacks."

7. Robert A. Bennett, "Black Episcopalians: A History from the Colonial Period to the Present," *The Historical Magazine of the Protestant Episcopal Church*, vol. 43, no. 3, September 1974, p. 240.

8. Ibid., pp. 242–43.

9. Cited by Chafe, *Unfinished Journey*, p. 319.

10. As quoted by James H. Cone, *For My People: Black Theology and the Black Church* (New York: Orbis Books, 1984), p. 37. Cone provides an invaluable history of Black theology.

11. Quoted in Warner R. Traynham, *Christian Faith in Black and White: A Primer in Theology from the Black Perspective* (Wakefield, Mass.: Parameter Press, 1973), p. 110.

12. Ibid., pp. 56–57.

13. For a critical assessment see Vine Deloria, Jr., "G.C.S.P.: The Demons at Work," *Hist. Mag. of the Episc. Church*, vol. 48, 1979, pp. 83–92.

14. I have taken this from "Report of the Committee of the… (Executive Council). Response to the Manifesto," August 29,1969, p. 2, in the Bayne Archives, General Theological Seminary, New York. See also Episcopal Church Archives RG 113.2–4.

15. John Hines and John Coburn to the *New York Times*, Sept. 8, 1969.

16. See Donald S. Armentrout, *Episcopal Splinter Groups: A Study of Groups Which Have Left the Episcopal Church, 1873–1985* (Sewanee, Tn.: The School of Theology, The University of the South, 1985).

17. Chafe, *Unfinished Journey*, pp. 364–65.

18. Langdon Gilkey, *Reaping the Whirlwind: A Christian Interpretation of History* (New York: Seabury, 1976), p. 13. See also William Barrett, *The Illusion of Technique: A Search for Meaning in a Technological Civilization* (Garden City, New York: Anchor Press/Doubleday, 1978), esp. pp. 20–22.

19. Jay W. Forrester, "Churches at the Transition Between Growth and World Equilibrium," *Zygon*, vol. 7, no. 3, p. 163.

20. *The Episcopalian*, April 1980, p. 1.

21. *The Blue Book*, Reports of the Committees, Commissions, Boards, and Agencies of The General Convention of the Episcopal Church, 1982, p. 177.

22. *The Blue Book*, 1985, p. 170.

23. *The Blue Book*, 1982, p. 174. See also *Jubilee Ministry*, No. 1, Spring 1983.

24. Cited in Carter Heyward, *A Priest Forever* (New York: Harper and Row, 1976), p. 87.

25. See Chafe, *Unfinished Journey*, pp. 328–35.

26. Ibid., pp. 440–41.

27. See Emily C. Hewitt and Suzanne R. Hiatt, *Women Priests: Yes or No?* (New York, Seabury, 1973), pp. 102–04, for a helpful chronology.

28. See Episcopal Church Archives, RG 3–49.

29. Report of a Special Committee of the House of Bishops, "On the Ordination of Women," House of Bishops document 72165, p. 19.

30. Ibid., p. 17.

31. Ibid., pp. 5, 7, 10.

32. Ibid., pp. 14–15.

33. For a helpful discussion of feminism and theology see Fredrica Harris Thompsett, *Christian Feminist Perspectives: On History, Theology and the Bible* (Cincinnati: Forward Movement Publications, 1986), pp. 35–48.

34. Rosemary Radford Ruether, *Liberation Theology* (n.p.: Paulist Press, 1972), p. 22.

35. *Journal of General Convention*, 1985, p. 198.

36. Ibid., pp. 605–06.

37. *Church Times*, March 14, 1986.

38. Ibid., March 21, 1986, p. 1.

39. Chafe, *Unfinished Journey*, pp. 278–80.

40. "The Religious Community and the War in Vietnam," a statement approved by the Executive Committee of Clergy and Laymen Concerned about Vietnam, February 1967, p. 2.

41. *Cross Before Flag*, Episcopal Statements on War and Peace, (The Episcopal Peace Fellowship, 1976), p. 3.

42. Ibid., 1967, p. 14.

43. Ibid., p. 15.

44. I am indebted to a paper by George J. Tompkins, written for a course on American Church History Since 1960, given by Donald S. Armentrout in the summer of 1986, for details concerning Lewis and the Williamsburg sermon.

45. *Cross Before Flag*, 1967, p. 3. I am grateful to Professor Armentrout for supplying me with his files on the Vietnam War and the churches.

46. *Journal of General Convention*, 1982, p. C–129.

47. Ibid., 1982, p. C–128; 1985, pp. 177, 206.

48. Ibid., 1985, p. 206. And see the extensive document on "Deterrence" submitted by the Joint Commission on Peace to the House of Bishops in October 1984, contained in the *Blue Book*, 1985, pp. 248–57.

49. *To Make Peace*, The Report of the Joint Commission on Peace (Cincinnati: Forward Movement Publications, 1982), pp. 7–8. First printed in the *Blue Book*, 1982, pp. 251–69.

50. Michael Hamilton, ed., *The Charismatic Movement* (Grand Rapids: Wm. B. Eerdmans, 1975), p. 7.

51. Kilian McDonnell, *Penance, Power, Praise*. Documents on the Charismatic Renewal, Vol. 1 (Collegeville, Minn.: The Liturgical Press, 1980), pp. xix–xx.

52. James W. Jones, *Filled with New Wine: The Charismatic Renewal of the Church* (New York: Harper and Row, 1974), p. 42.

53. McDonnell, *Penance, Power, Praise,* pp. 1–9.

54. Ibid., pp. 10–16.

55. Ibid., pp. 70–95.

56. Ibid., p. 96.

57. Hamilton, *Charismatic Movement,* p. 42.

58. McDonnell, *Penance, Power, Praise,* pp. 282–85.

59. For a description of a Roman Catholic Cursillo weekend see Marcene Marcoux, *Cursillo, Anatomy of a Movement, The Experience of Spiritual Renewal* (New York: Lambeth Press, 1982), pp. 65–97.

60. Philip Deemer, *Renewal Movements in the Episcopal Church* (Cincinnati: Forward Movement Publications, n.d.), p. 5.

61. Ibid., pp. 6–7.

62. See Marcoux, *Cursillo,* pp. 134–59. Some of the critique made by O.C. Edwards concerning "Evangelism in the Church" is relevant to Cursillo and Faith Alive; see Furman C. Stough and Urban T. Holmes, III, *Realities and Visions: The Church's Mission Today* (New York: Seabury, 1976), pp. 73–75.

63. John V. Taylor, *The Go-Between God* (Philadelphia: Fortress Press, 1973), pp. 17–18.

Chapter 3

1. William Barrett, *Death of the Soul: From Descartes to the Computer* (Garden City, New York: Anchor Press/Doubleday, 1986), p. 77.

2. Mihajlo Mesarovic and Eduard Pestel, *Mankind at the Turning Point: The Second Report of the Club of Rome* (New York: E.D. Dutton/Reader's Digest Press, 1974), p. 19.

3. See Chafe, *Unfinished Journey,* p. 447.

4. In *Christians in the Technical and Social Revolutions of our Time,* J. Brooke Mosley, ed. (Cincinnati: Forward Movement, 1966), p. 104.

5. See the bishop's address, May 23, 1954, *Journal of the Forty-fourth Annual Meeting of the Convention of the Diocese of Olympia.* pp. 43–44.
6. From an essay to be published in *The Study of Anglicanism*, S.W. Sykes and J.E. Booty, eds. (London: SPCK, 1988).
7. Conference of Missionary Executives, July 29, 1963, Huron College, Ontario, Canada, ACC Archives, London, file box labeled "Missionary Executives Meeting."
8. In *Anglican Congress 1963*, Report of Proceedings, ed. E.R. Fairweather (Toronto, 1963), p. 18.
9. *Anglican Congress 1963*, pp. 129–30.
10. "Mutual Responsibility and Ecumenical Responsibility," *Prism*, no. 80, December 1963, p. 29.
11. See S.F. Bayne, Jr., *Anglican Turning Point* (Austin: Church Historical Society, 1964), p. 93.
12. See John Booty, *The Church in History* (New York: Seabury, 1979), p. 240.
13. In James W. Kennedy, ed., *Partners in Mission: The Louisville Consultation, 1977 (Cincinnati: Forward Movement, 1977), p. 91.*
14. Booty, *Church in History*, p. 202.
15. *The Time is Now*, Anglican Consultative Council, First Meeting, Limuru, Kenya, 23 February–5 March 1971 (London: SPCK, 1971), p. 41.
16. Ibid., pp. 41–42.
17. See Leslie Newbigin, *Foolishness to the Greeks: The Gospel in Western Culture* (Grand Rapids: Eerdmans, 1986), p.2, for a helpful discussion of these terms.
18. See *The Time is Now*, pp. 24–27.
19. Ibid., pp. 42–43.
20. Ibid., p. 43.
21. Ibid.
22. Quoted in Neil Lebhar and Martyn Minns, "Why Did The Yankees Go Home? A Study of Episcopal Missions: 1953–1957," *The Historical Magazine of The Episcopal Church*, vol. 48, no. 1,

March 1979, pp. 27–43. This article contains a detailed statistical analysis of the decline in Episcopal Church missionary work.

23. See the *Blue Book*, 1982, p. 388, and the *Blue Book*, 1985, p. 328.

24. *Crossroads Are For Meeting: Essays on the Mission and Common Life of the Church in a Global Society*, Philip Turner and Frank Sugeno, eds. (Sewanee: SPCK/USA, 1986), pp. xliv–xlv. And see *Blue Book*, 1985, pp. 325–27.

25. As reported in *Bonds of Affection*, Proceedings of ACC- 6, Badagry, Nigeria, 1984 (London: Anglican Consultative Council, 1984), p. 48.

26. See Booty, *Church in History*, pp. 245–46.

27. See Bayne, address at a meeting of the Anglican Council of North America in Puerto Rico on "The Ecumenical Scene," Bayne Archives, D99.

28. *The COCU Consensus*, G.F. Moede ed. (Princeton: COCU, 1985), p. 1.

29. Ibid., p. 2.

30. See Anglican-Roman Catholic International Commission, *The Final Report* (London: SPCK and the Catholic Truth Society, 1982), pp. 1–2.

31. *ACC-5*, Anglican Consultative Council, Report of Fifth Meeting (London: ACC, 1981), pp. 42–43.

32. See Max Thurian, ed., *Ecumenical Perspectives on Baptism, Eucharist and Ministry*, Faith and Order Paper 116 (Geneva: WCC, 1983), pp. 197–224.

33. *Baptism, Eucharist and Ministry*, Faith and Order Paper 111 (Geneva: WCC, 1982), pp. 20–21.

34. *The Time is Now*, p. 3.

35. A working paper of COCU, 1965, prepared by S.F. Bayne, Jr., pp. 4–5.

36. *Final Report*, p. 6.

37. Ibid., p. 12.

38. Ibid., p. 30.

39. Ibid., p. 52.

40. Ibid., p. 86.

41. Mary Tanner, "The ARCIC Statements in the Context of Other Dialogues," *Their Lord and Ours: Approaches to Authority, Community and the Unity of the Church*, ed. Mark Santer (London, SPCK, 1982), p. 69.

42. Ibid.

43. *Salvation and the Church: An Agreed Statement by the Second Anglican-Roman Catholic International Commission* (London: Church House Publishing; Catholic Truth Society, 1987), p. 9.

44. See John M. Richardson, Jr., ed., *Making It Happen: A Positive Guide to the Future* (Washington, D.C.: U.S. Association of the Club of Rome, 1982), pp. 212–15.

45. Mesarovic and Pestel, *Mankind at the Turning Point*, p. 147.

46. Erwin Laszlo et al., *Goals for Mankind: A Report to the Club of Rome on the New Horizons of Global Community* (New York: E.P. Dutton, 1977), pp. 375–76.

47. Hugh Montefiore, ed., *Man and Nature* (London: Collins, 1975), pp. 73–75.

48. Ibid., pp. 77–78.

Chapter 4

1. A.M. Ramsey, *God, Christ and the World: A Study in Contemporary Theology* (London: SCM Press, 1969), pp. 72–73.

2. J.A.T. Robinson, *Liturgy Coming to Life* (London: Mowbray, 1960), pp. 17–18.

3. Emil Brunner, *The Misunderstanding of the Church* (Philadelphia: Westminster Press, 1953), pp. 9–18.

4. Ramsey, *God, Christ and the World*, p. 106.

5. Ibid., pp. 107–108.

6. Franklin Young, "The Theological Context of New Testament Worship," *Worship in Scripture and Tradition*, ed. M.H. Shepherd (New York: Oxford University Press, 1963), p. 90.

7. See Karl Barth on this, *Church Dogmatics* IV/2, pp. 697–98.

8. *Lambeth Conference*, 1948, Pt. II, pp. 3–4.

9. Ibid., pp. 5, 6.

10. *Journal of General Convention*, 1970, p. 466.

11. Ibid., 1973, pp. 590–91.

12. Ibid., p. 594.

13. Ibid., p. 595.

14. Ibid., 1970, p. 468.

15. Ibid., p. 470.

16. Furman C. Stough and Urban T. Holmes, III, *Realities and Visions: The Church's Mission Today* (New York: Seabury, 1976), p. 179.

17. Ibid., p. 182.

18. Ibid., p. 183.

19. Kelley, *People of God*, p. 43.

20. *The Myth of God Incarnate*, John Hick, ed. (Philadelphia: Westminster Press, 1977).

21. *Incarnation and Myth: The Debate Continued*, Michael Goulder, ed. (Grand Rapids, Mich.: Wm. B. Eerdmans Publishing Company, 1979), p. vii. This volume contains papers, pro and con, delivered at a conference held at the University of Birmingham, in England, July 10–12, 1979.

22. Norris, "Interpreting the Doctrine of the Incarnation," *The Myth/Truth of God Incarnate*, The Tenth National Conference of Trinity Institute, Durstan R. McDonald, ed. (Wilton, Ct.: Morehouse-Barlow Co., 1979), p. 69. See also John Macquarrie, "Truth in Christology," *God Incarnate: Story and Belief*, A.E. Harvey, ed. (London: SPCK, 1981), pp. 24–33, for a discussion of three kinds of truth, historical, theological, and metaphysical or ontological.

23. *Journal of Religion*, Vol. 59 (No. 2), April 1979, p. 249.

24. Sykes, "The Incarnation as the Foundation of the Church," *Incarnation and Myth*, p. 119.

25. Ibid., p. 122.

26. Norris, "Interpreting," *Myth/Truth*, p. 73. Norris makes the point that "the doctrine of the Incarnation is a *process of interpretation,* one in which past experience and past understanding are at

once preserved and transformed by being appropriated in the context of new questions and new ways of seeing things." Ibid., pp. 73–74.

27. Ibid., p. 74.

28. Ibid., p. 78.

29. Sykes, "Incarnation as the Foundation," *Incarnation and Myth*, pp. 125–26.

30. Sykes, *The Integrity of Anglicanism* (London and Oxford: Mowbray, 1978), p. 4.

31. See Urban T. Holmes, III and John H. Westerhoff, III, *Christian Believing*, The Church's Teaching Series (New York: Seabury, 1979), p. vii. The statement by Jones appears in all volumes in the series.

32. William J. Wolf, ed., *The Spirit of Anglicanism* (Wilton, Ct.: Morehouse-Barlow, 1979), p. 186.

33. Harvey H. Guthrie, "Anglican Spirituality: An Ethos and Some Issues," *Anglican Spirituality* W.J. Wolf ed. (Wilton, Ct.: Morehouse-Barlow, 1982), p. 3.

34. Norris, "The People of Grace," *Theology in Anglicanism*, Arthur A. Vogel, ed. (Wilton, Ct.: Morehouse-Barlow, 1984), p. 105.

35. Sykes, *Integrity*, p. 88.

36. Skinner, "Ideology, Authority, and Faith," *Authority in the Anglican Communion: Essays presented to Bishop John Howe*, S.W. Sykes, ed. (Toronto: Anglican Book Centre, 1987), p. 35. See Skinner's, *The Meaning of Authority* (Lanham, Maryland, 1983), p. 6.

37. See F.D. Maurice, *Moral and Metaphysical Philosophy*, Vol. 1. New edition (London: Macmillan, 1872), p. xxvi.

Chapter 5

1. *Theological Freedom and Responsibility*, p. 70.

2. David Edwards in *The Honest to God Debate*, p. 18.

3. *The Episcopalian*, May, 1980.

4. Kelley, *People of God*, p. 32.

5. Trinity Institute, *Towards a Theology of Priesthood*.

6. In Wolf, *Anglican Spirituality*, p. 3.

7. Taylor, "Introduction: The Voice of the City," *Believing in the Church* (Wilton, Ct.: Morehouse-Barlow, 1981), p. 4.

8. Norris, "Interpreting the Doctrine of the Incarnation," pp. 73–74.

9. In Wolf, *Anglican Spirituality*, p. 4.

10. Taylor, *Go-Between God*, pp. 17–18.

11. George Herbert's poem, "Prayer I."

12. In Avis, "The Identity of Anglicanism," ms. p. 18, to appear in *The Study of Anglicanism*, S.W. Sykes and J.E. Booty, eds. (London: SPCK, 1988).

13. *Book of Common Prayer*, in all services of ordination, pp. 523, 535, 546–47.

14. Macquarrie, *Principles*, p. 374.

15. See *Anglican Congress 1963*, p. 18.

16. *Cross Before Flag*, 1967, p. 15.

17. Ibid., p. 14.

18. Hooker, *Works* (1888), 3:617.

19. Donne, *Devotions Upon Emergent Occasions*, Meditation 17 (Ann Arbor, Mich.: University of Michigan Press, 1959), pp. 108–109.

20. Mesarovic and Pestel, *Mankind at the Turning Point*, p. 147.

21. Montefiore, ed., *Man and Nature*, pp. 77–78.

22. *Final Report*, p. 6.

23. Macquarrie, "Structures of Unity," *Their Lord and Ours*, ed. Mark Santer (London: SPCK, 1982), pp. 115–16.

24. Ibid., p. 117.

25. Ramsey, *God, Christ and the World*, p. 106.

26. *Lambeth Conference, 1948*, Part II, pp. 5–6.

27. *Journal of General Convention*, 1973, pp. 590–91.

28. Stough and Holmes, *Realities and Visions*, p. 182.

29. Sykes, "Incarnation as Foundation," pp. 125–26.

30. In Wolf, *Anglican Spirituality*, p. 4.

31. Skinner, "Ideology, Authority, and Faith," *Authority in the Anglican Communion*, S.W. Sykes, ed. (Toronto: Anglican Book Centre, 1987), p. 35.

32. *Lawes*, V.56.7. The quotations are taken from *The Folger Library Edition of the Works of Richard Hooker*, W. Speed Hill, general editor, 6 vols. (Cambridge, Mass.: The Belknap Press of Harvard University Press, 1977—).

33. Robert Isaac Wilberforce, *The Doctrine of the Incarnation* (Philadelphia, 1849), p. 271.

34. Hooker, *Works*, (1888), 3:617.

35. A.S. McGrade, "Introduction to Book VIII," to be published in vol. 6 of *The Folger Library Edition of the Works of Richard Hooker*, ms. p. 52.

36. Ibid., p. 53.

37. See I.2.5. See also my essay, "The Judicious Mr. Hooker and Authority in the Elizabethan Church," in *Authority in the Anglican Communion*, S.W. Sykes, ed. (Toronto: Anglican Book Centre, 1987), pp. 94–115.

Index